D1431409

The Philosophy Of Freedom

"In that new way of living,
and new form of society, which
is born of the heart, and which
is called the Kingdom of Heaven, there are no nations, there
are only individuals."

Boris Pasternak——

THE PHILOSOPHY OF FREEDOM

By
ROBERT K. WOETZEL

WITH
A DISCUSSION AT
THE CENTER FOR THE STUDY OF
DEMOCRATIC INSTITUTIONS

1966

OCEANA PUBLICATIONS, INC.

DOBBS FERRY, NEW YORK

S.M.W.

To fight the good fight together . . .

AUTHOR OF

THE NUREMBERG TRIALS IN INTERNATIONAL LAW, 1960.

THE INTERNATIONAL CONTROL OF SPACE (in German), 1961.

THE NUREMBERG TRIALS IN INTERNATIONAL LAW, Revised Edition with a Postlude on *THE EICHMANN TRIAL,* 1962.

ACKNOWLEDGMENTS

I would like to express my gratitude to Dr. Robert M. Hutchins for providing me with the opportunity to write this work. I am deeply indebted for advice and inspiration to Dr. Jacques Barzun of Columbia University, whose ideas have been with me since college days.

My thanks also to my wife without whose help this book could not have been written; to the members of the Center for the Study of Democratic Institutions for suggestions and criticisms; and to the clerical staff of the Center for their assistance. And I would like to express my gratitude to the publishers, Oceana Publications, Inc., for their patient and careful cooperation.

RKW

CONTENTS

Outline of A Philosophy
of Freedom

PREFACE

This work on the philosophy of freedom has grown from a discussion on political philosophy held at the Center for the Study of Democratic Institutions in September 1964. At that time the author stipulated that the starting point of a political philosophy that reflects the times must be the individual. Assuming that government must derive its authority from the consent of the governed, and since individuals make up the body politic, their consent is required for the exercise of authority. The determining element is freedom of choice. Any power which interferes with this freedom can only corrupt. The principle expressed is a relatively simple and familiar one; yet its implications have rarely been fully understood.

The experience of the past fifty years has shown that totalitarianism has constituted a real threat to world peace and an affront to human dignity. In creating a social order which will insure for all men "the right to life, liberty and the pursuit of happiness," regardless of race, color or creed, it is necessary to guard against the excesses of state control by guaranteeing civil liberties and individual rights. Though certain pressing problems are met by collectivist means, the common good is best served by insuring maximum individual freedom of choice within the framework of the *polis*. The aim is the balanced man who is willing and able to fulfill himself in harmony with society and through his own initiative in interaction with others: he is truly individual and social; he is a MAN in the Greek sense.

The discussion that followed centered on national and international problems. It was my personal view that the United States has a great destiny, if it furthers the principles of the philosophy of the free man. The realization of the principles of freedom, however, does not depend on any one country; rather, it is the work of individuals everywhere. Greater human dignity and freedom can only come through the cooperative efforts of peoples in all countries. Freedom so interpreted does not confine itself to any one country. It covers in broad outline the whole gamut of problems facing humanity today, and in its essence, it lays claim to universality. As Jefferson stated, freedom is indivisible; and the philosophy of freedom is applicable everywhere.

This work does not attempt to provide detailed remedies for all social and economic problems. Such a task would be beyond the scope and ability of the author. It is rather an effort to provide an approach to discussion. It is across the board in its criticisms and emphasis. It tries to balance different interests in terms of the common good. Most important, it attempts to provide a reference point for planning. In comparison with other philosophies which emphasize a particular solution to social, economic and political problems, the approach of a philosophy of freedom is inclusive rather than exclusive. The quest for freedom is underscored as a worldwide phenomenon. And it indicates in broad contours limited solutions to problems through the mechanisms of government, which will aid men in this quest.

The philosophy of freedom does not provide utopian visions. It works with the facts of life. It is understood that under certain circumstances individual freedoms must be restricted and this work describes such circumstances and the degree of restriction permissible. But it stresses over and over again the need to orient oneself by the objectives of freedom. Problems of freedom must be solved from case to case as they arise. Planning for progress is essential; but individual problems of freedom must be met. Only in this way can peace with freedom and justice be insured.

The common good and general welfare are assured through respect for human rights and human dignity. Freedom from arbitrary restrictions on human rights is essential for the realization of this philosophy. It is to be hoped that this contribution will serve as encouragement for greater citizens' action which is the price of freedom in our time.

RKW

Santa Barbara, June 1965.

INTRODUCTION

The aim of this exposition is to provide an outline of a political philosophy that expresses the aspirations of today's world and presents a framework that may fit its needs. It represents the faith of the author in the ability of mankind and the American people to cope with the political, social and economic problems that sap the strength of society. Man's capacity for growth, his ingenuity, encourage the enunciation of a hopeful theory.

The discussion will concentrate largely on governmental problems, those that concern the issue of central authority and the dispersion of power; the claims of the community versus individual human rights; the challenge of modern technology versus standards provided by inherited economic institutions, and the implications of nuclear weaponry versus the continued conflict of interests between nations. The underlying thesis is the continuing theme of the individual quest for self-fulfillment; man's striving for social order can only be understood in terms of each individual human being's efforts to achieve balance and harmony in society. Too often political theorists predicate the individual good on the common good which they imagine can be derived from some theoretical framework. In this discussion the common good will be established on the individual good, taking into account the need for social intercourse as well as the primacy of the interests of the person as distinguished from the state. In other words, government is instituted for the individual members of the body politic, and any governmental organization, local, national and international, derives its justification only from this basic proposition. Governmental frameworks, blueprints, and even the most brilliant theories have no other function essentially than to serve the collectivity of individual citizens. It is then the doctrine of the individual in society, his place, functon and responsibilities, that this theory describes and explains in terms of the issues we face today.

The concept of personal freedom is not new. However, certain political philosophers such as Marx, Mosca, Pareto, Michel, not to speak of Hegel and Rousseau bypassed this basic aim of all human striving in their attempts to find overall solutions.[1] Rousseau, for example, believed that man became equal "by convention and legal right . . . . The right which each individual has to his own estate is always subordinate to the right which the community has over all."[2] The writers of the *Federalist Papers* understood the meaning of personal freedom, when they rejected the authoritarian philosophers of earlier centuries and the tyrannical institutions of monarchy in favor of an approach that addressed itself to the immediate needs confronting the settlers in the thirteen states at that time.

Today the problem of individual freedom knows no boundary. Men must learn to recognize that their welfare depends on respect for the civil rights and human liberties of their neighbors. Economic problems, social needs, political and govermental issues become meaningful only in terms of the human dilemma. And this dilemma must be understood in terms of the aspiraitons, sufferings and happiness of individuals. There is no such thing as a collectivity without regard to the interests of each member. The Nazis believed that the tree was important, not the branches;[3] but individual freedom predicates that the tree is the union of all branches. Each branch matters. A moral approach that emphasizes the welfare of every single member of the body politic can be developed into a humanitarian instrument for progress. The author rejects the thesis that only the analysis of groups or classes or abstract entities and instruments of government can provide answers to the social, political and economic needs of people. He affirms the sacred obligation of every member of the world body politic to seek solutions

---

[1] See, for example, G. W. F. Hegel, *Philosophy of Right*, S. W. Dyde's translation, Section 260.

[2] Jean Jacques Rousseau, "The Social Contract," *The Political Writings of Jean Jacques Rousseau*, Vol. I, Chap. IX. Edited by C. E. Vaughan, Cambridge, 1915.

[3] A. Hitler, *Mein Kampf*, New York, 1939. p. 595.

to the pressing problems of our time by recognizing and helping his neighbor in need. This is the starting point.

Even as these words are written the upheavals in Russia's leadership, the changes in the Eastern European Communist dictatorships, and before that the passing from the world scene of the Fascist and Nazi regimes affirm the truth of the assertion that a crack in a mammoth is more dangerous than an eddy in a fluid mass. Democracies may not have provided the most efficient answers to economic and social problems at all times; but they have been able to bridge the difficult straits into which the dictatorships had plunged them while the latter perished. The reason is that man's nature supports the concept of individual freedom. All too often, however, members of democracies have weakened and despaired, because they were either not fully aware of the principles upon which the edifice of their state rested, or were reluctant to accept responsibility for necessary community action. For example, the consensus in the Weimar Republic was undermined by a lack of faith in democratic institutions. An attendant purpose of this work will be to clarify the governmental framework of democratic societies, as a means of strengthening the democratic consensus.

The edifice of the state thus rests on a political doctrine clearly enunciated and widely understood, and a consensus reflecting the will of the people to support and promote the ideal of greater freedom for all. The rational formulation of principles in terms of needs can mobilize such a consensus. It will constitute the basis for a free interaction of forces. Criticism serves as a stimulant to discussion. Through the interaction of different ideas in the framework of a free society the best may be produced, and such interaction depends on respect of the neighbor's right to speak, write, and associate freely. Thus, this political philosophy should also provide the starting point for creative discourse.

Outline

Of A

Philosophy

Of Freedom

1

INDIVIDUAL RIGHTS AND THE FUNCTION OF GOVERNMENT

Man and Society

THE aim of every man is happiness according to the standards which he chooses, and this may or may not involve the full development of his gifts and talents. The means that men choose toward the end of happiness may be explicit or implicit. They may become clear as a result of their action; or they may be stated as guidelines. Some men have a genius for intuition; they find their standards as a result of experience and seek to perfect them through the process of living. Most men, however, require a more clearly defined framework for action. They may, for example, profess a religion or political faith or follow certain ideals. These are usually highly placed, and consequently, achieving an approximation of them serves as a lifelong challenge.

Men usually require social relationships for their happiness. Only a very few are able to exist without much human company. The challenge of finding one's own end is complicated by others; for an individual's happiness largely depends upon the happiness of his neighbors. His own goal must, therefore, be related to his fellow human beings' striving for self-fulfillment.

At the same time man's social relationships are often the cause of difficulties, for, where interests diverge and rivalries occur, conflict develops. The nature of these rivalries can

1

be economic, social, religious—in fact, in any area of human endeavor. Philosophers of power like Thomas Hobbes have maintained that strife and conflict are common to human relationships.[4] This would be overlooking the fact, however, that experience and reason itself teaches that strife diminishes human happiness, and since man's basic striving is directed toward greater happiness, war and conflict must be regarded as contrary to the natural fulfillment of man. In this sense Pasternak stated that if force were the rule of life, the whip of the dompteur in the circus and not the cross of Christ would be the symbol of the ages.[5]

Nevertheless, much of man's history is concerned with the resolution of conflicts. In our time the threat of nuclear war has made the solution to the problem of peace a matter of human survival. Freedom today depends on interdependence. The free expression of the individual's will toward happiness must take into consideration the wills of others. Freedom of choice must be related to relative scarcity or plenty. Where there is conflict of choices, survival in our age demands adjustment and not conflict or suppression. Man's relationships in society must be based on interdependence in freedom.

╰The question might well be asked whether there is any freedom when scarcity or conflict imposes restraints on individual choice to the extent that very little variety is offered. The individual's quest for happiness in society must be *balanced*. It must fit in with the needs and possibilities of the community. Ideally speaking, the adjustment of different

---

[4] Thomas Hobbes, the great English philosopher of the mid-seventeenth century, maintains in his *Leviathan*, chapter 11, that "I put for a general inclination of all mankind, a perpetual and restless desire of power after power, that ceaseth only in death. And the cause of this, is not always that a man hopes for a more intensive delight, than he has already attained to; or that he cannot be content with a more moderate power; but because he cannot assure the power and means to live well, which he hath present, without the acquisition of more."

[5] Boris Pasternak, *Doctor Zhivago*. New York: Pantheon Books Inc., 1958.

individuals to each others' needs would provide the basis for a balanced society. The ancient Greeks regarded the achievement of such a balance between the interests of the individual and the *polis* as the end of society. The harmonious interaction between different wills and the balance of different interests was viewed as the pattern of the ideal society.[6]

If the story ended here, the solution to the human dilemma would be simple. But the problems of conflict resolution are endless; and it is often difficult to understand the will of individuals. Each man is different in nature and the adjustment of different interests is complicated. The prophets of love like Jesus Christ have counselled patience and restraint in the face of these difficulties. The reversion of man to force has convinced others that the clash of interests must inevitably end in war. And not that physical violence is the only form of war; the psychological mutilation of an individual's nature can be just as much of an example of the failure of man to achieve balance in society. The problem is compounded by the action and reaction of human beings in a conflict situation; force begets force, and before even the possibility of peace is explored, men are plunged into battle and bloodshed. The diversity of wills becomes the cause of man's unhappiness.

Taking the basic premise that man's end is his happiness according to the standards which he chooses, resolution of conflict of wills must be regarded as the primary challenge of the social sciences. The adjustment of human relationships so as to diminish conflict and increase the possibility of individual self-fulfillment must be the primary goal of a political philosophy for our day. This poses challenges both in terms of institutions and procedures. Institutionally, the standards which men choose must be designed to adjust different interests and lessen strife. Procedurally, the means

---

[6] Aristotle, *Politics*, transl. by Benjamin Jowett, in *Aristotle's Politics and Poetics*, New York: The Viking Press, 1957, Book III, Chap. 6.

chosen for adjustment of difficulties must correspond to the goal of individual self-fulfillment in a peaceful society.

The problems of discovering adequate standards must be related to the institutional needs of people. In this quest it must be determined whether or not there can be any definitive standards which apply to all people, and what the scope of such standards should be. How can standards for social inter-relationships satisfy the individual's quest for happiness according to his nature as well as the need for adjustment of different interests in a balanced society? The answer to this question will provide a solution to the problem of achieving the common good in a free society which takes into consideration the differences of human kind.

Philosophers from Plato to Marx have built their frameworks on the assumption that certain standards for the expression of human wills can be determined so as to apply to all men. On the other hand, anarchists of the nineteenth century opposed all government control, and economists such as Adam Smith believed with a kind of mystical faith that the free interaction of individual wills would produce the greatest good. Somewhere in between these extremes the philosophers of free societies like Jefferson, and especially the statesmen and architects of great commonweals like England, determined a framework within which a plurality of wills could exist without endangering the common good. Their conception of a harmonious society was broad, but at the same time protective. The United States as a union was created in order to insure "domestic tranquility" as well as individual rights. The political philosophy of the framers of the Constitution and the drafters of the Bill of Rights took into consideration the needs of the community in relation to the basic requirements of freedom.[7] Their framework acted as a restraint on those individuals who would abuse

---

[7] The Preamble of the Constitution of the United States aims at greater union as well as the preservation of the fruits of liberty.

their freedom at the expense of the common good. At the same time it guaranteed safeguards for individual rights against the encroachment of government.

The standards of a philosophy of freedom must be, broadly speaking, the guidelines of a social framework which allows for the maximum freedom of choice of individuals in relation to social needs. The aim of this framework is to permit each individual to fulfill his nature according to his needs. And to this end it imposes certain restraints which are necessary for the harmonious balancing of different interests. In brief, the ideal of man in a free society is diversity in unity.

The Function of Government

In earliest times man could deal with man directly, in order to solve any difficulties that arose between them. Communities, however, required some form of organization for the adjustment of differences. In ancient Greece the form was direct. The citizen could indicate his will by voting in assembly. The same was true for the New England town meeting. The growth of communities changed this pattern; it became necessary for the citizens to delegate to representatives the function of regulating communal affairs. Today evidence of direct democracy survives in the form of the plebiscite. Most countries, however, are governed by some form of representative system, and the degree to which the framework is truly representative determines the difference between authoritarian and democratic regimes.

The main function of government is to represent the citizenry in their communal relations. Ideally speaking, government should represent the will of each person in the community. Differences would be solved by maximizing individual freedom of choice. It is clear, however, that communal relations require that some claims be given priority over others. The standards used to determine the priorities reflect the deeper fabric of the society. And these have always been subject to experimentation.

Rousseau theorized that the people concluded a social contract upon which government was based. According to his *Article on Political Economy*, "The body politic, therefore, is also a moral being possessed of a will; and this general will, which tends always to the preservation and welfare of the whole and of every part, and is the source of the laws, constitutes for all the members of the state, in their relations to one another and to it, the rule of what is just or unjust."[8]

Marx regarded government as the reflection of economic conditions in a society. In his *Critique of Political Economy* he states that "In the social production which men carry on they enter into definite relations that are indispensable and independent of their will; these relations of production correspond to a definite stage of development of their material powers of production. The sum total of these relations of production constitute the economic structure of society—the real foundation, on which rise legal and political superstructures and to which correspond definite forms of social consciousness. The mode of production in material life determines the general character of the social, political, and spiritual processes of life."[9]

Democrats like Jefferson believed that government should express the will of the people: "Every man, and every body of men on earth, possess the right of self government . . . Individuals exercise it by their single will; collections of men by that of their majority; for the law of the majority is the natural law of every society of men."[10]

As viewed by these theorists, government was regarded as an instrument of service and protection for the community.

---

[8] Rousseau, *op. cit.*, pp. 241 *et seq.*
[9] Karl Marx, *Critique of Political Economy*, Preface, Eng. transl. by N. I. Stone, pp. 11 *et seq.*
[10] *Thomas Jefferson on Democracy*, New York: New American Library, 1953, p. 15.

Yet, in practice it has often become an instrument of oppression. The priorities determined by some have mitigated against the common good, and in instances government has negated the very purpose for which it was instituted. Instead of aspiring to adjust differences between individual citizens, it has on occasion become an end unto itself. In some societies governments have fortified the vested interests of minorities and in others they have been conducive to the tyranny of the majority.

[The real function of government is to adjust human differences so as to allow maximum freedom of expression within the framework of society.] This involves the protection of the community against attacks which would disrupt the social order and the establishment of certain services which facilitate communal inter-relationships and mitigate the hazards of social malfunction. This is especially true in modern society where technology and science have complicated social relationships to an extreme degree. Only a certain expertise can solve the problems that arise in modern society. Government today is indispensable for man's happiness; but this does not mean that government has any other *raison d'être* than to serve men. Planning, regulation, and control of social relations only make sense in terms of the welfare of individual members of the body politic. It is when government ignores this fundamental assumption, and government leaders assume an independent role in society that the rights of individuals are threatened. Priorities are likely to be determined according to the interests of the leaders and not the people. In the fascistic systems of government the power of the leaders is elevated into a supreme good.[11] In both fascist and socialist societies minority groups

---

[11] *Hitler's Words, the Speeches of Adolf Hitler from 1923-1943*, ed. by G. W. Prange, Washington: Public Affairs Press. See also Ernst Huber, *Constitutional Law of the Greater Reich*, 1939, who states that "The Fuehrer is the bearer of the people's will; he is independent of all groups, associations, and interests . . ."

and individuals are often suppressed, because they represent threats to the government.

While the priorities may not be ideally determined in democracies, they are often abused by leaders of other kinds of government. The monarchies of the sixteenth century refused to recognize the theory that political power belongs to the people and ruled by "divine right." Divine right was interpreted as a defense of order against what was considered to be the threat inherent in religious civil war. The theory was a modification of the accepted norm that authority had a religious origin and sanction. The oligarchy that governed France after the French Revolution was notorious for its abuse of rights. And in America, as de Tocqueville pointed out, the majority in certain communities tyrannized individuals.[12] The course of history seems to indicate that it is necessary to subject government to control in order to insure that it remains true to its original purpose. Government has a legitimate function in controlling various groups in society; but individuals must be protected against infringements of right by government as well as by groups or individuals who threaten the public order.

Democracy, or the rule of the majority with respect for the rights of minorities and individuals, tends to insure greater compliance with the wishes of more citizens than dictatorship by a group or an individual. But even democracy is not safe from the onslaughts of strong leaders who determine priorities of treatment according to their own interests. The function of government in a free society must be limited and its aim understood in terms of the interest of each individual citizen. Government then becomes an instrument of correction which is subject to the same safeguards as the groups which it seeks to regulate. The individual members of government are subject to the same

---

[12] Alexis de Tocqueville, *Democracy in America*, Vol. 1, New York: Vintage Books, 1959; see especially Chap. XV.

controls as other citizens. Government is not above the law. In the maelstrom of conflicting claims it becomes a contender on par with other power groups. This leaves the final decision in the hands of the citizens.

Whether or not government is fulfilling its obligations is a matter for each citizen to decide. Neither majority rule nor the power of pressure groups can substitute for the individual's judgment. Of course, it is not always possible to satisfy everyone. But then the aim must be to satisfy as many as possible with due regard to the rights of those who disagree. Under such a system the onus of responsibility lies with the citizenry. To function properly each member of the community must contribute to the general welfare. Where there is a slackening of interest or a separation of interests between government and citizen—a current danger when problems besetting government seem remote and generally too complex—there is a possibility that the balance wheel of control will be tipped by displays of excessive lawlessness or rigid arbitrary control.

In conclusion, it may be stated that the function of government is to help each individual citizen toward greater fulfillment of his personality. Modern technology and science make it possible for man to solve economic needs which previously were insurmountable. Government has powerful means at its disposal in the effort to diminish human suffering and assist men in their quest for happiness. The framework for government should allow individuals to experiment with different standards to that end; but under no circumstances should it allocate to itself the function of dictating standards for personal self-fulfillment. The leaders of a society may make recommendations; but in the final analysis, it is the individual who in his conscience must decide what road to take for his personal fulfillment. Those who doubt the ability of individual members of the body politic to choose for themselves have not learned that government which interferes with the fundamental rights of human beings breeds its own destruction. Whatever disasters may be caused by individual excesses, they can never equal the holocausts of modern totalitarian dictatorships of the right and left. There is no such thing as the common good without individual rights.

Law and Justice in a Free Society

It is the function of government to determine priorities in such a way as to serve the basic wishes of as many citizens as possible with due regard for the rights of those who might disagree. The selection of such priorities takes place according to certain principles and procedures anchored in law. Law in this sense, is the aggregate of principles, procedures, institutions, and practices which guide a society in the management of communal affairs. Individuals are both the subjects and objects of law; they determine legal standards and are governed by them.

Law like government has no other justification than to serve men. According to this conception, law must not interfere with individual choices unless it is necessary to protect the freedom of the many. In terms of the greater need, where such a choice is made the rights of the few must remain protected. Finally, laws should not serve as an instrument for the moral conversion of society according to any given standards, for men have the right to choose their own criteria for happiness and self-fulfillment.

On what basis are laws drafted? How are the legal standards which guide a community determined? Different nations have worked out complicated procedures for the drafting of laws. In a democracy the vote of a majority of the electorate or its representatives may be required for the formulation of laws. In communist states laws are determined by the representatives of the communist party. In England, parliament is the final arbiter of laws. In the United

States a complex system of checks and balances combined with separation of powers among three branches of government within a federal structure watches over the formulation of laws. In all instances certain *mores* and moral standards tend to guide lawmakers. They follow more or less explicit norms of right and wrong in determining the laws which guide a community.

Law can be said to be the reflection of these norms of conduct. If it is to be regarded as binding, it must conform to these standards. The understanding of justice may be local; but in the modern world conceptions of justice have become international.[13] Criteria of justice should guide lawmakers, and in so far as law conforms to standards of justice it must be obeyed. As the great international lawyer Brierly has stated, law is not just because it is binding; it is only binding when it is just.[14] And the Rev. Martin Luther King declared after receiving the Nobel Peace Prize that ". . . there are two types of laws. One is a just law and one is an unjust law. I think we all have moral obligations to obey just laws. On the other hand, I think we have moral obligations to disobey unjust laws because non-cooperation with evil is as much a moral obligation as is cooperation with good."[15]

Law is consequently not only command. It does not derive its authority from power. In a free society individuals are equal under the law which is designed to serve them all indiscriminately. Laws, however, can not satisfy everybody all the time. Nevertheless, the aim of law based on justice in a free society is to serve as many as possible with due respect for the rights of all. A violation of this principle constitutes a major premise for denying the validity of a

---

[13] Attitudes toward genocide and racial discrimination are two examples.
[14] J. L. Brierly, *The Law of Nations,* New York & Oxford: Oxford University Press, 1961.
[15] Statement by the Rev. Martin Luther King on N.B.C. program "Meet the Press," March 9, 1965.

law. A law which abrogates this standard to a substantial degree can be said not to be law at all; it is an abuse of justice.

When men follow the human quest for happiness and respect each other's rights, they will frame laws which serve and protect the citizens in their relations in the community. This process is violated when certain men set themselves up as final arbiters of the destiny of others; they then arrogate to themselves the function of making choices for their neighbors and determining standards for their happiness. In the Nazi and Stalinist dictatorships this development assumed major proportions, and minorities or so-called elites subjugated a majority in the name of false ideals.

Intelligent and worthy men have sometimes followed such ideals because they could not admit to themselves that there was no final and complete solution to the ills of society, and they wished to rid themselves and their fellowmen of the limitations of faith. On the other hand, their hopes and dreams were stimulated by those who perpetuated the ills of antiquated social and economic orders, and who in the name of tradition fortified the stratification of societies which benefited them. This interaction between extreme progressives, their direction notwithstanding, and reactionaries has been the bane of modern life. The plight of millions of underprivileged has been intensified by aggressive nationalism and the radical scheming of *avant-gardists* combating extreme reactionaries. The turmoil in Southeast Asia and Africa south of the Sahara, serve as current examples.

The theoreticians of Marxism and Leninism sometimes correctly predicted upheavals which they contributed to. Lenin and Stalin have been called geniuses in the organization of forces which employed violence and oppression, in order to hasten the so-called inevitable historical dialectic of revolution.

The leaders of democracies in modern times have tended

to combat this development by formulating safeguards which would prevent abuses of individual rights. They have launched the movement for human rights. In the United States efforts have been made, particularly by the Supreme Court, to protect individuals against the encroachments of the state and the community. In England economic legislation eased social imbalance; on the continent of Europe social reforms kept pace with citizens' demands. Constitutions of many states and international conventions like the European Declaration of Human Rights have enunciated the rights of man in society.

But while these developments have indicated the hopeful role of law in accordance with norms of justice, modern economy with its mass production, assembly lines, and increasing automation, have made it more difficult than ever for the individual to preserve his initiative and independence. The encroachments on his freedom have not been so much in the forms of tyranny, but in those social pressures which exist in a mass society that tend to deny him the kind of individual identity which in past ages allowed him to establish a small, but deeply satisfying personal circle of activity. At the same time the family has come under the purvey and censorship of the community.

Perhaps this development is unalterable; in his conscience man must still remain free. Law and justice demand that society assist him in his efforts to survive as a human being in a mass society.

Individual Rights and the Common Good

The purpose of government in a free society must be the common good which, ideally speaking, is the good of every individual member of the body politic. There is no abstract entity called the common good which is separate from the welfare of the individual members of the community. It is not always possible to fulfill the ideal, and differences be-

tween individuals compel government to give priority to
the wishes of one citizen against another in accordance with
law and justice. The aim, of course, is to satisfy as many
as possible without violating the rights of those who may
not agree. The problem confounding most societies is the
question of what rights are inalienable and how these are
to be safeguarded against encroachment by government.

While theoretically the rights of the majority are guaranteed in a democratic society, it has been difficult to determine in a definite sense the rights of minorities which should
also be protected. The history of the American Bill of Rights
as well as the French *Déclaration des droits de l'homme*
show that the contents of rights are always changing. The
U.S. Supreme Court has given preferential treatment to the
rights guaranteed in the First Amendment, but it appears
that under pressure of necessity even these rights may be
abridged. In periods of peace and tranquility the rights of
individuals are usually more safe than in times of national
crisis, when restraints may be imposed for the sake of national security or any other reason. In the United States
the rights of the Nisei Japanese were restricted during the
Second World War, and the Supreme Court upheld the jurisdiction of the Federal Government.[16] On the other hand,
the court attempted to restrain the Federal Government in
its exercise of powers during the Civil War.[17] While certain
Justices of the Supreme Court have taken a broad view of
the rights of the First Amendment, freedom of speech and
freedom of the press, for example, are not unrestricted.
Libel laws affect the latitude of expression both orally and
in print.

In authoritarian societies the power to abridge rights of
individuals is vested in governments. But in democracies a
certain consensus of the population is required for such

---

16 *Korematsu v. United States,* 323 U.S. 219, 223 (1944).
17 *Ex parte Milligan,* 4 Wallace 2 (1866).

action. In England and the United States the final determination lies with the electorate. The representatives of the British people acting in parliament can empower government to impose certain restrictions in times of crisis; but they may withdraw this permission, if they see fit. In the United States, Congress may authorize the President to declare a state of emergency during which the rights of individuals may be curtailed. However, through the election process or by constitutional amendment the electorate may indicate its wishes. Persons in a free society, therefore, have a greater control over the government's power to impose restrictions upon the rights of individuals than people who are governed by authoritarian regimes.

Nevertheless, the history of American legislation shows that the rights of individuals and minority groups can be severely curtailed by the majority of citizens, as in the case of the American negro. This is what de Tocqueville was referring to, when he spoke of tyranny of the majority. Such tyranny may also take the form of social pressure. In the United States, the rights of minorities and non-conformist individuals are protected to a considerable extent by the Bill of Rights. Only by an amendment to the Constitution may these rights be abridged. In England, a popular consensus tends to protect minority groups and individuals. The democratic theory of government, therefore, acts as a restraint on power. John Locke indicated that government could never arrogate to itself more powers than were granted to it by the free choice of the people. By free choice he referred to the majority: "That which acts any community, being only the consent of the individuals of it, and it being necessary to that which is one body to move one way, it is necessary the body should move that way whither the greater forces carries it, which is the consent of the majority."[18]

---

[18] John Locke, *Of Civil Government*, Book 2, Sect. 96.

John Stuart Mill spoke out against the abuse of individual rights by society, the acts of public authorities being but one aspect: "But reflecting persons perceived that when society is itself the tyrant—society collectively over the separate individuals who compose it—its means of tyrannizing are not restricted to the acts which it may do by the hands of its political functionaries: society can and does execute its own mandates, and if it issues wrong mandates instead of right, or any mandates at all in things which it ought not to meddle, it practices a social theory more formidable than many kinds of political oppression, since, though not usually upheld by such extreme penalties, it leaves fewer means of escape, penetrating much more deeply into the details of life, and enslaving the soul itself . . . There is a limit to the legitimate interference of collective opinion with individual independence, and to find that limit, and maintain it against encroachment, is as indispensable to a good condition of human affairs, as protection against political despotism."[19]

Jefferson predicated that the final authority should always be vested with the people, and if they failed on occasion to exercise their freedom of choice effectively, the solution lay in creating an enlightened electorate rather than in delegating greater power to government: "Whenever the people are well-informed, they can be trusted with their own government. Whenever things get so far wrong as to attract their notice, they may be relied on to set them to rights."[20]

Oliver Wendell Holmes described how the best guarantee for the triumph of good reasoning in a free society lay in preserving the "free trade of ideas."[21]

---

[19] John Stuart Mill, *On Liberty*, Chapt. I, pp. 138-139, in *Man and the State: The Political Philosophers*, ed. by Saxe Commins and Robert N. Linscott, New York: Random House, 1954.

[20] Jefferson, *op. cit.* p. 160.

[21] *Abrams v. United States*, 250 U.S. 616, 630 (1919).

These examples show that both the reason and the ideological commitment of persons who believe in freedom favor the conception that individual rights should not be restricted without the consent of the people. As Burke stated, when government controls appear necessary the question that citizens must ask themselves is how little not how much control is required: ". . . it ought to be the constant aim of every wise public counsel to find out by cautious experiments, and rational, cool endeavors, with how little, not how much, of this restraint the community can subsist."[22]

Conflict between individuals may have to be resolved by government action; but the aim must always be to enhance maximum freedom of choice for all. Even if crises require temporary restraints on civil liberty, such as during war, the purpose is still the same. A community may have to wage war in the defense of its fundamental rights; but a democracy does so with the aim of preserving liberty and freedom of choice. The experience of the U.S. Office of Price Administration in the Second World War showed that restraints on individual freedom had to be lifted once the crisis passed. Restriction on liberty can never be an end unto itself; it must be a means toward the end of greater liberty for all.

It is clear from this description that the common good is closely associated with the preservation and enhancement of individual freedom. This is so, last not least, because the conception of the dignity of man demands that the person be able to fulfill himself according to the standards which he chooses. The tyranny of one man over another abridges this fundamental conception. Ideally, men should be enlightened enough to pursue their goals in harmony with each other. Unfortunately, however, certain conflicts

---

[22] *Burke's Politics*, ed. by R. J. S. Hoffman and P. Levack; New York: Alfred A. Knopf, Inc., 1949, p. 109.

can not be resolved without the assistance of government. Law and justice safeguard the process which government serves and protect the common good by helping individuals solve their problems in society, and this involves a certain modicum of restraint. No one should be forced to subscribe to a program that is not necessary for the effective functioning of the social apparatus.

The limit of governmental authority is the line of demarcation between what can be legitimately called the public sphere and private areas of activity. This is so, because the function of government is to assist individual citizens in their communal relations, not to order their private lives. As unsatisfactory as the private choices of some citizens may appear to others, there is no remedy for such individual drawbacks other than persuasion. Force and authority can never take the place of liberty of choice in a free society.

2

INDIVIDUAL FREEDOM AND
MECHANISMS OF GOVERNMENT

The Problem of Centralization of Power

HAVING considered the dual role of government in terms of service and protection, the next problem to be considered is what form or mechanism of government best fulfills these functions in a free society. The best theory can be nullified by inadequate or ineffective procedures.

The centralization of power in the hands of a few mitigates personal freedom. Despots and oligarchs of past ages, and the present, could not often resist the temptation of dictating general and personal standards to their subjects. In the Middle Ages it was not permissible for persons living in the Holy Roman Empire to openly express a different religious sentiment from Catholicism. In the sixteenth century Henry VIII of England suppressed Catholic dissent. In the late eighteenth century the leaders of the French Revolution attempted to exterminate the aristocratic opposition. And in our time Hitler and Stalin purged their real or suspected enemies ruthlessly and without regard to fundamental conceptions of human rights. The more control was centered in the governmental authorities, the greater the devastation wrought. Modern dictatorships especially, have at their disposal terrifying and insidious means for keeping check on the citizenry and restraining any opposition. It is not necessary to visualize the authoritarian repression described in George Orwell's *Nineteen Eighty-Four*, in order to grasp the implications of extreme centralized government.

The usual cause for the centralization of power during different periods of history was a crisis that necessitated strong action. It would be wrong, however, to conclude that any single pattern emerges from a study of history which inevitably holds true. Today the degree to which government can observe and intimidate the citizenry has never been equalled before. In past ages it was always possible for non-conformist individuals to hide or emigrate, and they had a fair chance of survival. The dilemma of the German Jews caught between Nazi persecution and the reluctance of states to grant them asylum demonstrates the terrifying proportions to which government has grown and the helplessness of individuals in the face of this situation.

It is pointless to lament this development; the growth of government power has in large part been necessitated by the economic and political crises of this century. Governments have in increasing measure assisted millions of citizens in finding solutions for their economic problems. It is clear that in the less industrialized countries only a government which coordinates effectively the efforts of different groups can solve the outstanding economic and social problems. When millions of people are living at below subsistence standards, it is mandatory for the community to ration the goods of the society in such a way that fundamental human dignity and the right of every person to life at least is safeguarded. More advanced countries too are suffering from problems, such as in the educational field, which can only be solved through coordination of efforts. Big government is a by-product of the living conditions of our age.

The natural tendency of peoples, however, is to opt for less governmental control, when the crisis conditions which gave rise to government planning and caused an extension of governmental authority, are no longer acute. In the western democracies the pattern is borne out by events taking place in England and the United States since 1918: Americans voted for a decade of "normalcy" after the crisis of the First World War had passed; they confirmed the government programs and planning of President Franklin D. Roosevelt in the thirties, which followed the stock market crash of 1929; and after the Second World War the United States experienced a return to a philosophy which emphasized less government control under President Eisenhower. Today it would appear that the electorate favors a certain degree of government planning which does not unnecessarily interfere with individual freedom. In England a similar pattern prevailed until the Second World War, which was followed by a government that introduced large-scale planning, in order to relieve economic and social insecurity among the population. During the fifties the British experienced a return to less government authority and control under the Conservatives. At the present time the Labour Party again has a mandate to introduce new social and economic reforms.

It is important to observe in this pattern that freedom of the individual is closely related to his economic welfare. Freedom from want, as Franklin Roosevelt put it, is as important a concept of liberty as freedom of speech and freedom from fear.[23] The freedom to survive is obviously essential, and in the face of threats to life other freedoms recede in importance. When the belly of a man meets the backbone, he asks few questions about ideology.

Two factors emerge which are of importance for an understanding of the problem of centralization of power in our

---

[23] See Atlantic Charter: ". . . that all the men in all the lands may live out their lives in freedom from fear and want . . ." In Charles Fenwick, *International Law*, New York: Appleton-Century-Crofts, Inc., 1948, Appendix C.

time: great economic and political crises necessitate strong government action which usually leads to an increase of government control and authority, and when the crisis has passed less government control is favored. Politicians usually follow the mood of the people by advocating greater or less planning and government programming in accordance with the needs of the society at any given time. Relating this situation to the basic aims of man in society and the functions of government, it can be concluded that an increase of government power during a period of need may be justified in terms of the greater fulfillment of man; the individual's freedom may be curtailed by circumstances beyond his control, and only government action can insure for him a minimum of protection. Without such action his very right to life might be endangered. Nevertheless, the purpose of government in a free society must not be broadened beyond necessity.

Finally, the problem of centralization of power has been complicated by the increase of means of communication. Barriers between peoples have been broken down and interests of all peoples broadened. By increased social and economic interaction it is now conceivable that governments may exercise a degree of control over large regions. Even if we were to have world government, however, the previous observations would still hold true; for in order to prevent abuses of centralization of power, it is necessary to guard against the extension of government power on any level or in any place beyond the need for safeguarding fundamental human rights.

Federalism and Local Rights

The problem of centralization of power relates directly to the dispersion of authority in the governmental mechanism. Different points of decision-making enable the citizen to appeal his case with different authorities. Evident in this design is the fear of a centralized law-giver who dominates the political spectrum. Idealists like Rousseau assumed that a social contract could be worked out between the government and the people which would make the interests of one synonymous with the other. They were, therefore, willing to trust government as long as it reflected a popular basis of support. Marx theorized that in a proletarian society government would reflect the interests of the working class. Both the experience of the French Revolution of 1789 and the Russian Revolution of 1917 have shown that government becomes a force unto itself regardless of the circumstances under which it was conceived. The triumvirate of Danton, Marat and Robespierre was overthrown, because it did not and could not realize the *volonté générale* (general will). The Soviet government has become a "new class" which, according to the official admission of the Twentieth Party Congress, did not always represent the interests of the people. The reason for these failures is that government like any other institution of society, is made up of individuals who differ in their needs.

Government in a free society takes its place as a pressure group trying to win popular support for its programs like other major forces in the community, such as business, labor unions, and the fourth estate. Political parties too influence government and are in turn influenced by pressure groups. Theoretically, competition between different forces in society acts as a safeguard against monopolization of power; errors and misconceptions are weeded out in the process. John Stuart Mill, therefore, maintained that liberty was necessary so that truth might prevail: "Complete liberty of contradicting and disproving our opinion is the very condition which justifies us in assuming its truth for purposes of action; and on no other terms can a being with human faculties have any rational assurance of being right."[24]

---

[24] John Stuart Mill, *op. cit.*, pp. 154-155.

And Oliver Wendell Holmes remarked on the free trade in ideas as an essential attribute of a free society. The interaction then of different forces, including government, provides the individual citizen with maximum opportunity for expression of his choices.

Federalism is a mechanism of government which disperses power between different centers of authority in a particular country.[25] In the United States these centers are established in different states; and local communities also retain a certain degree of autonomy. The same is true for the Federal Republic of Germany and other nations with a federal system of government. The aim of federalism and local government is to allow the individual citizen access to points of decision-making which are close to home. In this way he retains the greatest possible control over government. The theory is that local authorities will be responsible for solving local problems, state governments for handling state affairs, and the federal government would coordinate services on the national level. This has been called the functional approach to federalism. The citizen's needs would be satisfied by the governmental authority under whose jurisdiction his problem may at any given time fall. Furthermore, problems which fall under different jurisdictions may be dealt with by different authorities. Government which is closest to a particular problem has priority of jurisdiction, and the next removed authority in the hierarchy should deal with it only after the lower level of authority has had an opportunity to solve the question. In this way, government by officials far removed from the problem is kept to a minimum. This arrangement of authority is commonly referred to as the subsidiarity principle.

---

[25] Federalism may not only involve geographic entitities, but can also refer to economic interests which form in effect private (or subsidiary) governments, e.g. A.T. & T. The balancing of these interests is one of the most important tasks of modern federalism and affects local, state, national and even international government.

In the experience of nations, "absentee government" has had almost as pernicious effects as absentee landlordism on the interests of the citizens most directly concerned. The more removed the government authorities are from local problems, the more likely are they to impose regulations on a community against the wishes of its inhabitants. Obviously, the interests of the local community must be balanced with the interests of other communities in the nation; but the starting point in this process of adjustment must always be the community and not the nation.

Critics claim that the federal system of government is unwieldy and leads to paralysis. There are, of course, democratic governments, Great Britain, for example, which are not federal in character. But even England has experienced Welsh and Scottish movements for home rule; and the dispersion of power between different groups in the British body politic is as complete as the division of authority between local, state and federal governments in the United States. Britain is a much smaller geographic entity than the United States, and this tends to lead to greater cohesion of governmental mechanisms and the party system. The homogeneity of English society is another factor which may account for greater centralization.

It is understandable that in a heterogeneous society like America, for example, a wide dispersion of power between different localities would be practiced. The danger of conflict between different points of decision-making must, however, be taken into account in this system of government. The provincial interest might clash with the national interest. Furthermore, local communities may not always respect fundamental human rights as they are recognized elsewhere. The racial problems in the United States indicate that for certain minorities local and state government can amount to a denial of justice and the equal protection of the law. The federal government in this country has clashed repeatedly with local and state jurisdictions in the South on this issue. National action has given rise to claims of unlawful interference. Should government close to home prevail, even if fundamental rights are denied thereby?

Local and states' rights, as well as the rights of the federal government must always be related to the basic aims for which governmental mechanisms and organizations in the states have been established, namely the welfare of the individual citizen. If any mechanism of government, be it local, state or federal, interferes with this fundamental objective, it would be denying its very purpose for existence. It is clear then that conflict between different governmental jurisdictions as well as between individuals and the state must be solved with this objective in mind. The government authority which denies individual rights and civil liberties must be restrained in the interest of freedom. In such a situation the federal safeguards work in reverse: the federal government may have to restrain local or state government. The aim nevertheless remains the same: maximum freedom of the individual in society. Federalism like any other form of government is only a means to that end.

The Right to Revolution and the Doctrine of Interposition

Governments are instituted to help man to attain his end of greater happiness and self-fulfillment. The Declaration of Independence provides that when government no longer serves this purpose, it is the right of the people to "alter" or "abolish" it. Furthermore, in the United States certain "residual powers" are vested in the states, which the federal government may not abridge. The question now posed is whether citizens have the right to revolt, if government does not fulfill its legitimate purposes and abuses fundamental freedoms.

It is possible to conceive of the obligations or duties of citizens in terms of the functions of government. To the extent that government requires the cooperation of the citizenry in discharging its duties, individual citizens may be considered obligated. Citizens' duties, therefore, derive from the *necessities* of government. There is no inherent obligation of citizens to government in the abstract sense. Citizens' duties become clear from case to case; they are clarified in the decision-making process.

The rights of citizens may, however, be considered "residual." Decisions should be left to the individual unless he needs the services of government on any level. As Abraham Lincoln stated, government should not do for the people what they can do for themselves as well or better. The abrogation of the rights of any individual like the interference with the wishes of any person must be justified by necessity. In case of doubt, the burden of proof rests with the government. *In dubio pro reo.*

The rights of individuals assume paramount importance in a free society; they must constitute the basis for political action. There can be no more serious transgression than a violation of individual rights. In a mass society where means of control by government have been refined to an advanced degree, vigilance is more than ever the price of freedom. When government violates the end for which it is instituted by violating the rights of individuals, the citizens are free to alter or abolish it. This does not mean that people can exist without government under our present conditions. The Marxist conception of "withering away of the state" has proved nothing more than fiction in the light of communist experience. But people have the right to institute new governments, if the old ones violated their purposes, so that government may fulfill its legitimate function.

The right to revolt is, thus, clearly stipulated. People have the right to rebel, if the government violates basic human rights. They have the right to contravene government authority and to disobey laws which do not represent a legitimate exercise of power. Rules and regulations imposed by governments in violation of fundamental human rights and civil liberties are not binding; law must be just in order to be binding. Laws which are not just are tyrannical, and tyranny must be resisted.

This raises an important additional factor: the right to revolution includes the right to "abolish" a government. This may involve the slaying of a tyrant or tyrannicide, though the act might be hard to justify on moral grounds. However, it is clear that the plot to assassinate Hitler in July 1944 was well justified by the transgressions of the Nazi government.

It is dangerous to the stability of a society, if any individual citizen can decide that a particular law or government is unjust. The "underintegrated" societies of Latin America have been shaken time and again by revolutions which were not always necessary. Here as in the judicial process, gravity is of the essence. The threat to liberty and individual freedom must be substantial before it is possible to speak of tyranny. An occasional transgression, lamentable as it may be, does not constitute an overwhelming threat or a "clear and present danger" to the freedom of the people. Latin American revolutions were often perpetrated by individuals who were seeking power rather than greater freedom. The right to revolution must be substantiated, therefore, and the transgressions of authority have to be clearly manifest.

Modern international criminal law supports this conception when it stipulates an obligation on the part of citizens and especially government leaders to resist illegitimate and tyrannical exercises of power which are grave and recognizable to any person. Such transgressions constitute violations of "general principles of law recognized by civilized nations."[26] The right to revolution is, therefore, anchored in a human tradition which is world-wide and goes to the very core of human existence. Man, wherever he may be, can recognize such violations as heinous abuses of his dignity and free choice. He can not be expected to live under such conditions. His right to revolt becomes necessary for his survival as a human being. Anything less would be the basest form of slavery. To aid and abet the process would be criminal.

The subsidiarity principle stipulates that each level of goverment, local, state or federal, should only deal with problems which the lower level can not handle. In other words, government power builds up from below and should not be imposed from above. Authority filters through from individual citizens in interaction with each other. In contrast with dictatorial, authoritarian doctrines, the philosophy of freedom emphasizes the right of each individual citizen to influence and control government directly or indirectly. Central government organs which violate the principle of delegation of powers in a federal system can be said to be interfering with the freedom of expression and the right to control of individual citizens. If a grave and manifest transgression of local or states' rights takes place, local or state authorities have the freedom to take measures to counteract this infringement of basic liberties. The right of citizens in the states to revolt against federal government control has sometimes been referred to as the doctrine of interposition. During the Civil War the Southern states claimed the right to interpose between the federal government and the people.

It is important, however, to remember that states' rights like federal rights do not serve as an end unto themselves; they too, are instituted for the greater happiness of indi-

---

[26] Statute of the International Court of Justice, Art. 38 c, in Fenwick, op. cit., Appendix E.

vidual citizens. The test of interposition is whether the exercise of states' rights is necessary for the survival of individual freedom. In the case of the Southern states of the United States this was obviously not so, since interposition would have meant the perpetuation of slavery which is contrary to fundamental conceptions of law and justice.

Toward a World Order

In most modern political philosophies the functions of government are described as twofold: government is to legislate and regulate for the benefit of the community, and at the same time, safeguard individual rights. In practice, a great deal of confusion has resulted from this division which often appears to represent a dichotomy in standards. Government planners have considered this separation of functions as a mandate to proceed in the communal area with their policies and programs while leaving the protection of civil liberties and individual rights to other authorities such as the courts. Consequently, violations of rights have occurred as a result of administrative discretion. On the other side, it is true that defenders of the Bill of Rights have sometimes ignored the necessities of government. A political philosophy should combine the functions of government in such a way as to serve one standard of values instead of two or more. The conception outlined here aims at a philosophical unity which preserves the element of diversity.

Law and order are conceived of as the necessary corollaries of human action and communal interaction. They are required for the full expression of the individual. By guarding individual citizens against unwarranted infringements on their liberties, government fulfills essentially the same function as when it serves any member of the body politic. Its restrictive function is no more or less than an extension of its service role. Government is serving human

rights both when it restricts someone whose actions constitute a real or threatened injury to another citizen, and when
it serves individual citizens, since the aim and occasion for
the exercise of authority restrictively and permissively is
the same.

In the world community today various countries are governed by authoritarian regimes; others can be described
as democracies; and some contain features of both. The
Soviet Union, for example, is an authoritarian dictatorship.
The United States is a constitutional democracy. And France
under the Fifth Republic contains features of strong centralized government combined with guarantees of human
liberties as are customary in free societies. With such variety
the question that naturally follows is whether some degree
of world order is possible.

Governmental mechanisms are in some ways reflections
of modes of behavior. In a national community persons
with different temperaments learn to cooperate with each
other, when this is required for their common good. The
principle on which a free society is based is diversity in
unity. Why should not the same principle be valid for the
peoples of the world? It is true that authoritarian-minded
persons may endanger the peace of the community by their
aggressive actions; but then the challenge in the international as in the national sphere would seem to lie in establishing rules and procedures which would safeguard human
rights against such aggressive behavior. Obviously nations
do not act like individuals; but the individual in the world
community is becoming more of a subject and less of an
object in modern international law. Individuals may, therefore, be considered the true carriers of sovereign power in
the world. Individuals interacting in national communities
may consequently be the subjects and objects of a future
world order.

World order thus conceived is a system of rules and procedures which maximizes the benefits of communal action for individuals everywhere by essentially recognizing their rights and diversity. Man is deserving of this attention wherever he may live and under whatever circumstances. The diminishment of world barriers has made the globalization of a philosophy based on freedom of the individual both possible and necessary. In the face of nuclear war, cooperation between states with different governmental mechanisms has become a *conditio sine qua non* for the survival of mankind. The most advanced development of international law and United Nations action in such areas as human rights indicate a growing understanding of the place of the individual in modern society.

The aims and aspirations of governments cooperating with each other on different economic and social projects must be directed toward the greater happiness of human beings everywhere. The movement for human rights, especially in Europe, has endowed individuals with greater power to express their choices and to appeal to different points of decision-making in the international sphere. The European Commission of Human Rights and the Court of Human Rights are stars on the horizon of this progress. World order like national order must serve individual human beings. International planning, therefore, must also take into consideration the rights of individuals. It is thus hoped that the recognition of the function of international government in these terms will lead to an intensification of the movement for human rights.

While the international community does not yet possess the power for imposing sanctions against aggressors in the way states can restrain criminals, the theory described here would endow the organs of the international community with authority for the protection of human liberty. The war crimes trials at Nuremberg are signs of such a development. The officials of every nation must now be aware that they too may be condemned as international criminals, if they offend against the law of nations, instigate or prepare wars of aggression, apply laws that are in violation of the laws of humanity, or persecute groups or persons whose rights are recognized by most civilized nations.

Today it may also be necessary to impose sanctions on violators. *Apartheid* in South Africa is a case in point. The restrictive as well as the permissive function of international government derives from the same *raison d'être*: the role of government to assist individuals in their quest for happiness according to standards which they choose. In the international community as in the nation an understanding of this fundamental principle may lead to greater freedom and an enhancement of human dignity.

3

HUMAN RIGHTS AND HUMAN DIGNITY IN THE MODERN AGE

Human Rights and Human Dignity

THE despotism of the monarchs of the sixteenth and seventeenth centuries led to widespread demand for equality in the late eighteenth century. The French Declaration of the Rights of Man and the American Bill of Rights are examples of this development.

In our time the movement for human rights has become international; the United Nations Declaration of Human Rights affirms the will of the international community to protect persons everywhere against unwarranted infringements of their liberties. In Europe today it is possible for the citizen of one country to appeal against the authorities of his nation before an international tribunal. The Lawless case in which Lawless, a citizen of the Republic of Ireland, petitioned the Commission of Human Rights in Strasbourg against his government is a case in point.[27]

The demand for protection of human rights has usually grown more intense after a period of dictatorship. This is especially true for the developments of the twentieth century in which the democracies have been twice involved in major conflicts with authoritarian governments. The suffering caused by war and the suppression of human rights

---

[27] *Lawless v. Republic of Ireland*, European Commission of Human Rights, in *American Journal of International Law*, Vol. 58, 1964, p. 396.

in dictatorships gave impetus to movements for human rights after World Wars I and II. The democracies also experienced a curtailment of individual rights during these periods; national service, rationing and other wartime measures were imposed.

The link between movements for human rights and periods of crisis can be found in the concept of human dignity. The horrors of trench warfare during World War I and the massive devastation wrought by World War II detracted from human dignity to an unprecedented degree. The cry for protection of human beings against war grew stronger as a result. The movement for the outlawry of war in the nineteen twenties which culminated in the Kellogg-Briand Pact is one end product and the Nuremberg trials of war criminals, another.

During war military machines usually take full control of the manpower and resources of a nation. Such control may be modified in the democracies when civilian leaders remain at the helm of government; but generally speaking, under conflict situations, the character of government tends toward authoritarianism. It is most extreme in the totalitarian dictatorships, and the history of the Nazi and Soviet imperiums bear testament to acute human suffering.

War and authoritarianism are causes for the decline of human dignity, and the two are related in our time. In the twentieth century countries like Holland and Denmark where individual freedom has flourished have not been aggressors, while Nazi Germany and Soviet Russia, among others, were condemned for aggressive actions by the international community. The major democracies also have not been without defect; the influence of the military and the power of centralized government have increased to unprecedented degrees during period of crisis. A decline or diminution of regard for individual rights and human liberty, wherever it occurs, has usually been accompanied by violent transgressions of human dignity.

In dictatorships transgressions of human rights take place not only during wartime, but in peace. The barbarous and inhuman treatment of prisoners in the German concentration camps was not a wartime phenomenon; it began shortly after the Nazis seized power. Similarly, the Stalinist purges did not take place during wartime but several years before World War II. The Russian author Solzhenytzin describes suffering in a Siberian labor camp in his *One Day in the Life of Ivan Denisovich.* The arrests and killings of the Castro regime in Cuba or the practices of the recent Trujillo regime in the Dominican Republic are but two more examples. On a larger scale the imposition of *Apartheid* by the South African government is a blatant disregard for human rights. It should also be noted that in a democracy like the United States authoritarian police practices may diminish human dignity by violating human rights; examples of such violations can be found in the Southern states particularly. Authoritarianism, whether practiced on a systematic basis in totalitarian dictatorships or in communities by the local police, is a cause for the decline of human dignity.

The violations of human rights in Nazi Germany before World War II showed that transgressions of human liberty can lead to major conflict. The International Military Tribunal at Nuremberg decided that such violations of the laws of humanity taking place in wartime could be prosecuted like war crimes. As a result, the international community today is concerned with violations of human rights as potential causes of war. It is no coincidence that the outbreak of many a conflict has been preceded by charges and counter-charges of brutality and violation of the rights of the citizens of one country or another. The violation of the rights of a majority of negroes and racially mixed people in South Africa under *Apartheid* may be regarded as a potential source of conflict. The nations of Africa have warned that the continued brutalization of racially related population groups in South Africa as well as Portuguese Angola might lead to war. The government of the newly independent Zambia has threatened to aid insurrection in Southern Rhodesia where racial discrimination is practiced. The government in South Africa like that of Nazi Germany, claims that its racial policies are of no concern to the international community since they fall under its jurisdiction. Under the Nuremberg principles, however, a plea of domestic jurisdiction can not be entered, if the action of a government constitutes a crime against international law. According to the Judgment of Nuremberg, grave and flagrant violations of human rights may be prosecuted as crimes against the law of nations. And this Judgment was unanimously endorsed by the United Nations—giving tangible evidence of the validity of these principles.

Finally, it is necessary to examine the relation between the movement for human rights and an understanding of freedom in terms of the concept of human dignity. The basic objective of a philosophy of freedom is to secure to man maximum freedom of choice in the exercise of certain inalienable rights. By inalienable rights we mean those rights that are necessary for man's development and fulfillment. Their contents are constantly undergoing change as humanity attempts to adapt to changing conditions. The deeper and more profound basis of this philosophy must be found in the concept of human dignity. Theories and instruments of government are only means to that end. As strange and aberrational as a man's behavior may seem to his fellow citizens, he has a right to the exercise of his freedom as long as his actions do not constitute real or threatened injuries to his fellow human beings.[28] As different as a man might seem, he has, in the words of James Baldwin, the right to

---

[28] See American Law Institute, *Model Penal Code*, 1962, for definition of crimes.

[29] James Baldwin in his play *Blues for Mr. Charlie*, 1964.

walk the earth as a human being.[29] This is the nexus; this is the starting point and the end of all government. Political philosophy, therefore, to be relevant, must be based on the concept of human dignity; and in that cause it should become a safeguard for the greater fulfillment of human rights.

Suppression of Rights in Modern Societies

Human rights have been violated in various societies; but such transgressions have been especially devastating in our time. The inventive genius of man has become an instrument of death and destruction and the full arsenal of modern technology has been utilized for the debasement of human dignity and the exploitation of man by man. The mere contemplation of a repetition of the destruction wrought by World War II can only bring despair.

Violations of human rights in modern societies do not, however, occur in isolation. They are often the result of conditions and attitudes which have been nurtured through centuries. A combination of factors contributed to the phenomenon of Nazism. The same is true for Stalinism and other forms of authoritarianism. Man used the ingredients of his society to build the holocaust; he appealed to traits which were deep-rooted and exploited needs which had become chronic and acute.

In explanation it may be helpful to examine in detail certain incidents of suppression of rights in recent times. In the Soviet Union the Stalinist autocracy was built on many precedents in Russian history. From the time of Ivan the Terrible and even before, through the reigns of Peter the Great, Catherine the Great, Alexander the First, the ill-fated Nicholas II, to the Bolshevik leadership of Lenin and Stalin autocrats have governed Russia. In fact, the title "Autocrat" was officially assumed by Czar Ivan who married Sophia, niece of the last Byzantine Caesar, Paleologus. This long history of autocracy combined with serfdom which existed until the late nineteenth century contributed to a kind of fatalistic acceptance of dictatorship by the Russian people. This feeling was strengthened by the acquiescence of the Russian Orthodox Church which today prays for the health of the atheistic members of the Soviet Presidium as it once did for the Czars. It is not surprising, then, that the Leninist principle of democratic centralism should have turned out to be more centralistic than democratic. While the Soviet Constitution guarantees federalism (Articles 13, 14, 15, 19, 20, 105, 123 and 133) and even the right of "secession" (Article 17), and "the people" theoretically possess the right to choose their representatives, the Soviet Union is, in fact, a dictatorship with the Communist Party Central Committee at its helm and through most of its history an autocrat presiding over the whole machinery of the state. As the Soviet Twentieth Party Congress discovered, autocracy and "the personality cult" of Stalin led to the most heinous violations of human rights.[30]

The authoritarianism of the German leaders during the Nazi period also had many antecedents. Since 1648 the rulers of German principalities played an almost autonomous role, wielding power over their subjects. Unlike England or France, Germany did not really experience a violent bourgeois uprising against the aristocracy and monarchy. The pattern of power was monolithic in most of the German principalities. It was extreme in East Germany where serfdom continued to exist until the nineteenth century. In 1848 the German bourgeoisie demanded certain reforms which were met shortly afterwards by the aristocratic rulers. Again, unlike England or France, compromises between the German aristocracy and the rising bourgeoisie were reached without much accompanying violence. There was no equi-

---

[30] In this connection, the parallels to Stalin in the Soviet regisseur Eisenstein's great film work *Ivan the Terrible* have been widely commented on.

valent in Germany to the terror of the French Revolution. This monolithic pattern was extended after 1860 to the rising working class which after initial cries for reform was mollified by Bismarck's social security services, and as a result had acquiesced in his suppression of the Social Democratic Party. The abdication of Bismarck and the return of the Social Democrats to the political scene led to certain initial successes of the working class party at the polls; but the outbreak of World War I saw the Kaiser proclaiming that "I know no parties; I know only one German people."

As a result of the German defeat in World War I, the Social Democrats came to power. Reich President Ebert, however, was far from a militant working class leader once he assumed authority. In German native jargon, the Social Democratic leaders could not divest themselves fast enough of their working garb, in order to put on the burgher's tails. In spite of resounding socialistic slogans, the Social Democrats had become bourgeoisiefied.

When the Nazis appeared on the political scene as a power, the German workers' leader, Boeckler, after some initial resistance tried to make his peace with Hitler. The result is well known: the workers' movement was suppressed by the Nazis who substituted their own cell organization under Robert Ley. German authoritarianism in the twentieth century can be partially explained by this historical evolution. German critics of this development have referred to the so-called "Radfahrerkomplex" which makes the German bow to his superiors while he tramples all beneath him. The lack of an effective opposition was the primary root of the evil. The Federal Republic of Germany is attempting to correct this situation by allowing for the freedom of expression customary in democracies.

Authoritarianism, however, can take different forms. As noted previously, it need not be exercised by a dictator or an oligarchy; it can be the result of social pressures that impose a conformity on groups or individuals against their will. The witch hunts of Salem, the Alien and Sedition Acts, and the McCarthyite persecutions of the early nineteen fifties are examples of tyranny by social pressure reinforced by public authority. These incidents were over the long haul repudiated by the American people; but they constitute warning signals of a special kind of authoritarian streak which is peculiar to America. One cause may be the conformistic puritanism practiced in the early history of this country. Intolerant moralism still leads to denial of rights. Private "immoral" conduct, for example, is still subject to penal sanctions in many states. It is clear that this kind of oppression can be especially insidious, since the victim is isolated and his fellow citizens shun association with him.

Other examples of the denial of rights in modern societies are the inhuman exploitation of cheap labor by landlords and managers in some of the less industrialized countries, the perpetuation of poverty in the slums, and most flagrant of all, the denial of due process and the equal protection of the laws to racial minorities. In each case power is wielded unscrupulously either by an individual, or a group, or by government. The challenge of a political philosophy for our time based on human dignity lies in finding safeguards against such abuses.

Protection of Rights in the Future

Too often false political conceptions have served as the rationale for violations of human rights. Thus the Nazis thought that they were serving a "higher ideal," when they purged the Jews and other so-called "asoziale Elemente" (anti-social elements), such as gypsies and homosexuals. Former Prime Minister Khrushchev of the Soviet Union once ran about the floor on all fours shouting "I am the locomotive of history." The leaders of the French Revolution thought that they were fulfilling the popular will, when they instituted their regime of terror. In most of these cases the leaders believed that their decisions were identical with the will of the people. Robespierre once said of his Jacobins, "Our will is the general will." The school of thought that began with Rousseau stipulated an ever growing affinity between the leaders of a movement and the people they purported to represent. In one of his speeches Hitler declared "I am the people." Similarly, but in a different context, Louis XIV of France had once stated "l'état c'est moi." It is interesting to note that these claims were usually made by one party to the "social contract," namely the ruler. This is in striking contrast to the Athenian democracy in which ultimate authority was vested in a popular council of citizens.

It has been pointed out that the separation of the functions of government in terms of service to the collective and protection of individual rights can lead to confusion. In a free society both functions are related to the same aim, namely the enhancement of human dignity through maximum freedom of choice. In the same sense, traditional distinctions between rights and duties of rulers and subjects can be misleading. Governments do not possess any rights *per se*; obligations of individual citizens derive from the necessities of government, but government serves their rights and not *vice versa*. The dichotomy between *populus* and *princeps* can be resolved, therefore, by referring back to the ultimate authority, namely the people. Unlike Hobbes who would impose *Leviathan* on the body politic, this approach would follow both Locke and Burke in denying to government any authority beyond the powers delegated to it by the people.

In view of the experience of authoritarian and autocratic dictatorships, it would be simple-minded to identify the governmental decision-making process *ipso facto* with a popular consensus. The abstract notion of popular will is not very helpful; only the relation of governmental powers to individual rights can resolve the dilemma created by a conflict between government and the people. The courts, the executive, and the legislature are involved in this clarifying process, and power is exercised in interaction with the people. The popular consensus, if there is such, becomes clear through interaction of the different forces in society. The popular will is not an abstract conception; it becomes the will of the individual members of the body politic. This development coincides with a growing recognition of the place of the individual in the international community and in international law.

Theories which proceed from the rights of government to a supporting consensus must be regarded as essentially undemocratic. They intend to impose governmental power according to "expectations of reciprocity," which is another way of saying administrative discretion. These philosophical rationalizations are dangerous, to say the least; they have served to still the consciences of aggressors and criminals throughout history. The political fanatic seeks for such a rationale, in order to feel justified in the exercise of his powers. Eichmann, Wolff, and Boger, among others, "believed" in the Nazi program. As attractive as these theories may seem to the radical or utopian reformer, a close look at the results should convince any impartial observer that political philosophy must begin with the rights of individuals and end with the happiness of individuals rather than with the rights of governments and the happiness of the collective. What, after all, is the collective, but a conglomeration of individuals?

The protection of human rights in the future requires the implementation of declarations of rights. A philosophy which in its fullest sense is dedicated to the concept of the dignity of man, can be used to counteract false authoritarian images like "purity of race" or "inevitability of class struggle."

The institutional framework of a free society will be discussed in detail in the second part of this work. It is enough to say for the present, that one of the greatest enemies of human progress has been the ideologue with a vision in his eye and a sword in his hand. Ideas are like seedbeds for action. It is necessary to combat authoritarian ideas in whatever guise with the same dedication and conviction, which have characterized the efforts of their originators. Alfred Rosenberg, the author of *Der Mythus des 20. Jahrhunderts,* was not only Hitler's theoretician, but administrator of the conquered regions of Russia. In that capacity he "distinguished" himself for the most ruthless implementation of his theories. In a way, ideological war has always been most brutal; the conflicts of the Thirty Years' War and the American Civil War were extremely bloody. It would be wrong to conclude, however, that it is better to acquiesce in a false ideology than to challenge it. A stronger stand on the part of the democracies against Hitler's aggressive designs, when he sent his legions into the Rhineland, might have prevented the outbreak of World War II. As unhappy as the alternative may seem, ideological warfare is the only answer to the challenge of aggressive ideology. A political philosophy based on human rights and the concept of human dignity is the best answer to the aggressive ideologies of our time.

4

ECONOMIC AND SOCIAL PLANNING IN
A FREE SOCIETY

The Need for Planning

Adam Smith in his *Wealth of Nations* maintained that by following natural economic laws—what he later called the "obvious and simple system of natural liberty"—the greatest prosperity and harmony is produced. Or as David Ricardo put it, "the pursuit of individual advantage is admirably connected with the universal good of the whole." *Laissez-faire* capitalism operated on these assumptions during the nineteenth and early twentieth centuries. Its main incentive for progress was the profit motive.

Social critics of the period considered this situation intolerable as the abuses of expanding industrialism were leveled against the workers. Marx elaborated a theory in which capitalism became the answer to the economic challenge of the industrial revolution while socialism would succeed capitalism in the new age as capitalism had succeeded feudalism. Since the Bolshevik Revolution various countries have adopted the socialist model. Government planning took the place of the market mechanism. In Russia, Lenin proclaimed his plan for electrification. All branches of the economy were subjected to planned supervision. Cultural and social activities were directed according to plan. The result was forced industrialization within a relatively brief period of time.

In other countries the market mechanism persisted with certain modifications and controls. The profit motive remained as the major incentive; but gains became increasingly subject to governmental restrictions. In the United States today the economy is a mixture of government regulation and private enterprise. Franklin Roosevelt's New Deal introduced far-reaching reforms, which led in turn to large-scale planning in certain areas of the economy, such as banking, commerce, agriculture, etc. Government agencies have multiplied in our age, the largest single business being the Federal Government itself. The President's Council of Economic Advisers plans for fiscal and economic changes; the National Security Council plans for defense; and the State Department's policy planning staff formulates foreign policy. Wide-range planning is, therefore, not peculiar to the socialist economies; it exists in varying degrees in all countries today.

Scientific, and technological changes in our society have made some degree of regulation and coordination necessary. All large-scale private businesses such as the General Motors Corporation and the Ford Motor Company, take into account the trends of the national economy, when planning their activities. Certain industries, such as motor and steel, comprise a major portion of the private sector of the economy. In a mass society with automation and computer controls, planning in depth is essential for the maintenance of order and stability. It is not so necessary in smaller economic enterprises. Even in the Soviet economy certain minor enterprises were exempted from nationalization. Today especially, the less industrialized countries in Asia and Africa find overall planning necessary in order to stimulate economic growth. In most of these countries hunger and starvation are real problems; a piecemeal approach would hardly suffice, when the needs are so great.

Planning will become even more important with the proliferation of problems as a result of the growth of the world population and the increasing challenges of modern science and technology on earth and in space. The United States and the Soviet Union are at this time trying to outplan each other in the space race. Major economic development programs, both national and international, are postwar phenomena; the United Nations and its network of agencies have been especially effective in aiding national and regional planning. Generally speaking, planning in different areas is now being related, and planning in the public and private sectors of the economy will be coordinated to an increasing degree.

In order to remain in control of the scientific and technological revolution he has wrought, man must fully use the products of his inventiveness. To do so effectively, he must continually be aware of his own purpose. The far reaching purpose of planning in a free society is the enhancement of human dignity by making available to men everywhere the benefits of modern science and technology. By planning the removal of slums and the raising of living standards in the poverty-stricken areas of the world, it may be possible to provide men with greater opportunities and, therefore, greater freedom. Man's energies can be released from the hectic quest to survive economically and redirected to such fields of endeavor which he may choose for his individual self-fulfillment. Projecting ideally, cultural and spiritual incentives may take the place of the economic profit motive. In such an age man will become increasingly the master of his fate. He will be able to seek his happiness according to the standards which he chooses.

An objection may be made, however, that the record of oppression in the Soviet Union and Communist China does not confirm the virtues of planning since planning has had dehumanizing effects in these countries. During the period of the Stalinist purges the individual was subjected to persecution and in Communist China forced labor has deprived millions of their freedom. Stalin's award system (accord) benefited the functionaries and penalized the mass of laborers and farmers who were theoretically, the sovereign carriers of the state. Not only in the Soviet Union and other Eastern European communist countries did this bureaucracy increase, but also in the Western democracies. Planning in some instances became a pursuit which benefited the planners. The greater the distance between the planners and the people planned for, the more likely were abuses to occur.[31] The isolation of the ruling elite in some countries contributed to their lack of understanding for individual problems. It is interesting to note in this connection that Marx never provided for an independent bureaucracy in his scheme.

Planning like any other form of governmental activity must be related to individual rights. Government decision-making can not be considered in the individual's interest unless it is the result of his need. The essential consideration is not whether planning benefits the whole of society, because to determine this would be extremely difficult even with the use of polls and statistics, but whether the individual members of the body politic need and want such planning. Unless a major crisis threatens a society and overall planning becomes necessary for survival, piecemeal planning, that is planning from case to case, would be a safer way on the whole of solving social and economic problems with due regard for individual rights. Political activity would insure that information as to individual needs reaches the planners. In this way the distance between planners and populace is lessened.

Limits of Authority and Government Planning

The main purpose of government planning consists of

---

[31] Examples of bureaucratic mishandling are legion in both the U.S.S.R. and the United States.

removing obstacles to the realization of citizens' rights. These rights span the whole spectrum of human activity. The right to freedom of expression, the right to freedom from want, the right to freedom from fear, among other liberties, must be safeguarded against unwarranted encroachments or denials. Government counteracts threats to individual rights by providing necessary services and protection.

Theories of planning often start with the function of government to solve the economic and social problems of the period. The political community is conceived of as an abstract entity; and planning becomes the instrument for the realization of the general will. The modern "social contract" is regarded as a mandate to the representative organs to deal with the challenges of the technological and scientific revolution in terms of the collective need. The British socialist theoretician Harold Laski and more recently, the writings of the American socialist Norman Thomas, bear out this emphasis. Planning is conceived of as decision-making of a political or judicial nature based on statistical estimates of future needs. The planners become the primary administrators of law and justice in the new society. They interpret the popular consensus in terms of popular needs.

The function of government in a free society, however, is not to prescribe planned solutions for a wide range of human activity. The individual members of the body politic may or may not agree to integrated planning in the political, economic, and social spheres. Government would only be justified in interfering with this freedom of choice, if real or threatened violations of basic human rights were involved. In such instances government would be protecting individuals against infringements of their freedom of choice. It may be necessary to employ police power and military force to safeguard such rights. A democratic concept of planning would, therefore, preclude coercive planning involving curtailment of certain rights when this is not necessary for the protection and enhancement of human rights generally.

It may be argued that planning in the education and culture fields, for example, is desirable, because it serves the general welfare. Should individuals be allowed to prevent such planning, when for one reason or another it does not coincide with their interests? The answer to this question provides the key to a reasonable differentiation between planning in an authoritarian society and a free society. Whether or not government planners may enforce their decisions on the basis of a majority vote or on any other grounds, against the wishes of individual citizens when there is no question of basic human rights involved, is the crucial problem.

In the Soviet Union plans are imposed on the people. In the Israeli Kibbutz, however, persons voluntarily agree to coordinate and plan their communal life. In the United States planned reforms are usually justified in terms of needs, Congress being the final determinant of their relevance. The Kibbutz may serve as a starting point in the differentiation between planning in authoritarian and free societies. When there is no overwhelming need or clear and present danger and individual rights or the protection of them is not a crucial issue, planning must be voluntary. Persons may decide to subject themselves to a socialist plan; but in a free society they can not be forced to do so.

Does this mean that the majority in a free society can not vote for certain desirable programs, though they may not involve services or protection essential for the preservation and enhancement of human rights? Not necessarily. A majority may vote for certain plans which are opposed by a minority. As long as these plans do not violate basic individual rights, they may be realized.[32] The point of distinction

---

[32] For example, cultural exchange programs, foreign aid, public education assistance, highway maintenance, public housing, medical assistance, etc.

is that plans which entail a loss of rights can not be imposed in a democratic society; they may be voluntarily accepted by persons. Plans which do not involve the violation of basic rights may be fulfilled if supported by a majority, even though they are not essential for the protection of fundamental individual rights, but are desirable from a social standpoint.

This means that enforced planning must either be voluntary or necessary for the preservation of liberty or desirable, but not interventionist. The limit to the authority of government planners is where individual rights are infringed upon. The line of demarcation is set where civil liberties and freedom are endangered. No amount of rationalizing will justify violations of rights, and only a grave or overwhelming need could make their curtailment necessary. The exposition of Stalin's crimes indicates that regardless of the economic progress made under his regime, nothing could justify his disregard for human life. His crimes are legend. Similarly, the challenges of the scientific and technological revolution can not be used as a justification for unwarranted infringements of individual rights.

In the final analysis, planning which is based on an acceptance of differences between individuals and a recognition of their special needs is more likely to serve the general welfare and the common good than coercive planning for an imaginary ideal. Planning that has disregarded minority rights as in Nazi Germany, as efficient as it might be, usually leads to catastrophe. Planned *Apartheid* in South Africa is as reprehensible as forced collectivization of the Kulaks in Russia. It is necessary in assessing the planning function of government, therefore, to stake out the limits of authority and to respect them under all circumstances.

Planning for Freedom and Greater Human Dignity

In modern mass society planning is essential for the implementation of human rights. Freedom from want can only be achieved through the coordination of individual and group efforts. Plans and programs based on past experience and estimates of future needs enable people to make fullest use of the benefits of science and technology. The haphazard, piecemeal "muddling through" of past ages is no longer possible; the needs of the world population can only be satisfied by the systematic setting of standards and concentrated efforts to achieve them. The maximum utilization of resources depends on coordinated planning assisted by modern means of fact gathering. Computer analyses and statistical information are invaluable aids in this process.

The aim of all planning is greater individual self-fulfillment. Economic planning in a free society must be directed toward safeguarding human rights and human dignity by freeing man from unjustified material restrictions. Freedom of choice can only be meaningful, if man's economic well-being is not threatened by starvation or annihilation. This does not mean, however, that government should necessarily dictate methods of production. Restrictions on economic enterprise can be justified in terms of need. The right to property like any other right carries inherent restrictions. The question to be asked is whether freedom from want or freedom of opportunity require such restrictions. Furthermore, the degree of restriction should be proportionate to the need. In that sense, government should not control any activity where regulation would suffice.

Human liberty may be restricted in the economic sphere by large combines. Huge corporations or labor unions can dominate an individual and deprive him of his freedom of choice as effectively as any government. One task in the practical application of the political theory in mind must be, therefore, the balancing of different interests in society so as to protect individual citizens against unwarranted infringements of rights by large combines. Private concerns may vie with representative organs of the community to promote their respective aims; but in this process the individual's welfare is still of paramount importance.

It may be feasible under certain circumstances to prevent huge conglomerations of financial and economic power in private cartels as well as in government. This is not the only solution to the problem posed by powerful pressure groups and big government. Greater control by the individual members of the body politic over economic and social organizations in the community by means of the ballot or popular movements or consumer associations, etc., may be a more effective way to prevent abuses arising from monopoly power. Most citizens belong to one pressure group or another, and everyone should be interested in controlling the organizations which serve the public need. The cry for reform in private industry or government usually arises as a result of extreme arbitrariness on the part of functionaries and managers. The main problem for freedom in the sphere of economic planning, therefore, is popular control over the plan and the planners.

In an age where economic problems do not constitute serious obstacles to personal happiness, the challenges of social and cultural activity will become of primary importance. Education and cultural efforts of one kind or another are of significance to the community as a whole. A certain amount of government planning may be necessary, in order to bring the benefits of education and culture to persons who would otherwise not be acquainted with such endeavors. The community may require coordinated planning in these fields. The aim of such efforts in a free society must be, however, the promotion of individual initiative in the cultural and social spheres as in any other area. Private programs and esoteric efforts should be encouraged along with publicly supported programs. The final test of the value of any particular cultural or social contribution must be the body politic. Education brings new insights to people; but the choice of a particular mode of expression should remain personal. This is in contrast to the practice of authoritarian societies which dictate a conformist standard to all citizens. Authoritarian communities may encourage cultural and social efforts; but these, in the final analysis, are subject to the veto of the supremely powerful directors of the state.

A philosophy of freedom is based on the notion of individual initiative. Generally, individual efforts are coordinated in a voluntary manner. Persons in a free society are able to choose to join or not to join any particular grouping. They can not be deprived of their choice of privacy or independence in favor of some utopian ideal; such enforced "happiness" has only led to oppression and conflict wherever it has been attempted. The experiment of the disciples of Plato to establish an ideal Greek state in Sicily was a dismal failure. It is not necessary to refer to the unhappy experiences of millions of Russians and Chinese dominated by a new power elite which professes a Marxist ideal, in order to demonstrate the truthfulness of this observation for the present. The philosophy of freedom predicates, therefore, that individuals be encouraged to find their own, distinct cultural and social pattern of development. This places great responsibility on the individual who must be aware of his choices.

It is often pointed out that many persons are not well-equipped for the task of cultural and social self-expression. If this is so, then no amount of dictation will solve the problem; all the coercive imposition of group standards can accomplish is a certain uniformity through conditioned response. In order to achieve the aim of helping individuals to find their personal happiness through cultural, social and economic freedom, it is necessary to provide cultural, social and economic incentives for self-development. These incentives may take material form; but they also can be of an intangible, spiritual nature. The important thing is that individuals are more likely to seek self-expression in the cultural and social areas, if they have been stimulated by the promise and prospect of self-fulfillment. An important task for modern education must be, therefore, the adaptation of general standards to the individual.

A society which makes use of its economic resources, cultural talent, and genius for social organization is best equipped to help individuals achieve greater human dignity. When the imminent prospect of starvation has been banished from areas where millions hunger today, and fresh hope born, then the search for beauty, the desire for deeper insights through learning, will become an inseparable part of the human quest for happiness. The dignity of man can be measured in terms of opportunity for the maximum use of his gifts and talents. The more man can and is inclined to develop himself, to criticize himself, to look searchingly at the challenges of his environment, and to rise above the narrow confines of his personal, individual situation by relating and communicating effectively to others, the greater the degree of human dignity in society. Human dignity and human opportunity are linked in the vision of a free society.

A philosophy of freedom looks forward to even greater achievements in science and technology for mankind's benefit; it is based on the conception of a society in which individuals fulfill themselves and help to fulfill each other through the quest for true beauty. "For we are lovers of beauty," as the ancient Athenians would say, which is another way of confirming the pattern of harmony that must be the goal of all economic and social efforts and of planning in our time.

5

INTERNATIONAL PEACE AND THE

STRUGGLE FOR FREEDOM

The Meaning of Peace

The late Soviet Foreign Minister Andrei Vishinsky once stated that war is not the only alternative to peace. He was referring to modes of conflict that do not involve a clash of arms. Soviet strategy has made use of various tactics, including military action and political and economic pressure. Conflict is a rule of nature, both human and animal. The struggle for survival is basic to man's quest. While competition is not the only way of resolving human differences, and cooperation is in many cases mandatory for man's survival, differences of human nature will inevitably result in some degree of conflict. The point is that means must be found to resolve conflicts which will enhance man's dignity and enable him to survive.

Jesus Christ, the great prophet of peace, indicated in many of His actions that the struggle for peace involves opposition to unpeaceful or anti-peaceful elements in society. The philosophy of freedom provides that freedom from the fear of war and war-like conflicts is essential for man's happiness. The purpose of government in a free society is to assist men in resolving their differences by peaceful means. In fact, the main function of government consists of balancing different interests so as to prevent unjustified infringements of rights resulting from aggression. Aggression in international relations as in personal affairs, is a major threat to the enjoyment of freedom. In modern times the drastic consequences of nuclear war make this assumption more valid than ever before. Freedom from war has become necessary for the survival of mankind.

The quest for peace then is two-fold: on the one hand, it is necessary for man to devise peaceful means for the resolution of conflicts, and on the other, opposition to war-like elements is necessary for his survival. Peace is not some kind of a *nirvana* in which men lose their differences and learn to cooperate without any difficulty; it is rather a dynamic, progressive state of affairs which requires constant attention, caution and care. In the final analysis, peace can not be attained without personal conflict and personal victory over the aggressive, imperialistic human instincts of man. One might almost say that peace is war in a sociological sense.

The meaning of the term peace lies in the goal sought and not in any abstract notion of a "peaceful world." If the aim is peace, then conflict becomes a struggle for peace. If the aim is some Nietzschian ideal of "superman" or the conception of the "dictatorship of the proletariat," then the process to attain such ends can be considered aggressive and war-like. The attempt to realize such objectives usually leads to war, as recent history shows. The Draft Code of Offenses against the Peace and Security of Mankind and the Declaration of Human Rights indicate that the pursuit of political and economic objectives of any kind must be subordinated to the aim of peace. The essential factor in all calculations must be the recognition of legitimate differences between human beings and the insistance on modes of behavior in international relations which will not endanger peace. This does not mean that the *status quo* must be "frozen" in order to attain peace: on the contrary, the quest for peace entails constant change. Thus Article 19 of the Covenant of the League of Nations provided for "peaceful change," and one of the major contributions of the United Nations has been to place a buffer between warring or contesting parties, in order to allow them time to resolve their differences peacefully.

Why is it that the term peace has been abused so greatly by those who insist that their conception of justice will bring order and attempt to impose it by force, if necessary? The coercive imposition of any conception of social justice is as contrary to the basic aim of man as it is in violation of the legitimate functions of government. Authoritarian conceptions provide for forced change and forced imposition of standards. Freedom and peace are inseparable in the philosophy of freedom, however. It is precisely to prevent unjustified attacks on individual rights and aggression against the liberties of men that a philosophy of freedom limits the role of government in society. The preservation of a maximum degree of freedom of choice is the best guarantee against aggression.

Mutual respect and non-intervention have become principles of international law. The whole development of law in the international sphere since 1945 confirms the basic assumption in international relations that peaceful change must not involve coercion. The growing importance of the individual in international law extends this protection from states to every citizen of the world community. Peace with freedom and justice becomes the goal of a new world order. Peace without freedom is as unthinkable as freedom without justice.

The world is no longer able to afford aggression and war. It perhaps never legitimized these modes of conflict. In other times the conception of "just war" did provide for certain limitations on the right of sovereigns to resort to arms for the resolution of conflicts; but in our day, men will no longer tolerate war for any reason, except self-defense and the enforcement of international law.

The pursuit of peace can be understood in terms of a never-ending struggle against unpeaceful elements in society and a challenge to remove those political, economic and social obstacles which are causes of war. With such an understanding it should be possible for men to devise means for the peaceful resolution of conflicts, not resorting to idealistic utopian schemes on the one hand nor acquiescing in artificial rationalizations of the use of force on the other. The preservation of peace becomes an eminently realistic enterprise; for without peace in this sense, no one would be secure in his freedom.

Peoples and Nations

Since the decline of the Holy Roman Empire nations have provided the rallying point for war or war-like efforts. In the nineteenth century legal theory invested the national sovereign with the supreme power to wage war. The theory of auto-limitation allowed the national sovereign to abolish any limitation on his right to wage war; since all sovereigns were equal, they could take back any restriction on their powers to which they might have consented. In previous times the exercise of the right to resort to arms was restricted according to the just war doctrine. Catholic thinkers like Vitoria[33] and Suarez[34] expanded on this doctrine in their works; the sovereign could not wage war unless certain prerequisites had been fulfilled: one, there must be just cause for waging war; two, the intention of the sovereign must be right; three, the power waging war must have legitimate authority; and four, there must be a reasonable chance of success. The confessors of the Church would advise the princes of the realm on the moral and ethical aspects of the doctrine. Although the dismemberment of the Holy Roman

---

[33] Franciscus de Vitoria, *De Jure Belli*, 1539, IV (In publication of Carnegie Endowment for International Peace, No. 7, Washington, D. C., 1917).

[34] Franciscus Suarez, *De Legibus*, L. II c. 19 (In publication of Carnegie Endowment for International Peace, No. 20, Oxford 1944).

Empire and the decline of the temporal authority of the Church diminished the practical importance of the just war doctrine, states continued to pay lip service to just war ideas. Immanuel Kant in his *Zum Ewigen Frieden* commented ironically on the tendency of sovereigns to argue ethics, when at the same time they would resort to almost any means in order to implement their plans.[35]

In line with the historical development of the nationstate, the Prussian philosopher Hegel identified the supreme good with the state, his final synthesis being the ideal state. In the first half of the twentieth century nationalism combined with totalitarian authoritarianism produced the most terrible holocaust of war and destruction; the idea of the nation-state became the vehicle for unlimited power, and modern dictators were able to mobilize the masses in the name of patriotism.

The claims of national sovereigns to represent the common good were usually based on the argument that the will of the leadership represented the general welfare. This identification of the will of government and the governed in terms of the power of the leaders is responsible for the kind of blurring of lines of responsibility which led to fanatical, blind obedience to criminal orders. The leaders could do no wrong in the eyes of the followers; as a result, they could impose the most ruthless and arbitrary forms of dic-

---

[35] See Immanuel Kant, *Zum Ewigen Frieden*, 1795, pp. 24-25 (Parnass-Library edition No. 37): "bei der Boersartigkeit der menschlichen Natur, die sich im freien Verhaeltnis der Voelker unverholen blicken laesst . . . ist es doch zu verwundern, dass das Wort Recht aus der Kriegspolitik noch nicht als pedantisch ganz hat verwiesen werden koennen, und sich noch kein Staat erkuehnt hat, sich fuer die letztere Meinung oeffentlich zu erklaeren; denn noch werden Hugo Grotius, Pufendorf, Vattel u.a.m. (lauter leidige Troester), obgleich ihr Kodex philosophisch oder diplomatisch abgefasst nicht die mindeste gesetzliche Kraft hat oder auch nur haben kann (weil Staaten als solche nicht unter einem gemeinschaftlichen aeusseren Zwange stehen), immer treuherzig zur Rechtfertigung eines Kriegsangriffs ange-fuehrt, ohne dass es ein Beispiel gibt, dass jemals ein Staat durch mit Zeugnissen so wichtiger Maenner bewaffnete Argumente waere bewogen worden, von seinem Vorhaben abzustehen."

tatorship on their people. The nation thus became the excuse for tyranny. The leaders grew more powerful with the acquiescence and active support of the populace, and the people became means in the implementation of the leaders' plans. Immanuel Kant's warning against the reduction of human beings into mere means went unheeded as government claimed the right to impose a conformistic pattern on all citizens. The diabolical nature of this identification of leaders and followers becomes most clear in the destruction of individual consciences. The Nazi war criminals believed that they were following an ideal, when they committed atrocities which their original background and upbringing should have told them were contrary to all standards of civilized behavior. Man mobilized by a power ideal was reduced to the state of a wild beast. His mind, his ingenuity, his education and culture became nothing more than instruments of crime. He was swept along by the movement of his time; he had lost his individuality; he debased his human dignity by committing inhuman actions.

Modern international law recognizes a distinction between governments in the abstract sense and nations and peoples as a collection of individuals with rights and responsibilities. Modern political theory too takes into consideration differences between government and the governed. Even the Marxists assume that when government does not correspond to the so-called "dialectic of history," the people must be distinguished from the leadership. In Soviet strategy and tactics this means to "divide and rule." The idea of the separation between government and the people, however, is valid. Government is only a means toward an end. Man, the individual, and man, the member of the social group, is the carrier of supreme power in the free state. The free state in

It is possible to speak of a law of peoples in our time. The philosophy of freedom is the basis of this law. Not nations but peoples are the arbiters of human destiny, and peo-

turn is only one mechanism among many for the implementation of individual wills.

ples living in freedom with justice are the hope for a peaceful world. The destruction wrought by fanatic nationalists must be counteracted by the healthy idea of the supremacy of peoples and individuals over government everywhere. In that sense, the world is one when peoples, not nations, are the end of international planning for peace.

Interdependence and International Peace

Since 1945 the danger of a nuclear holocaust has compelled all governments to seek peaceful solutions to major conflicts. This does not mean that war has become obsolete; but war which could lead to nuclear retaliation is regarded as impractical by most governments. The Communist Chinese at this time do not admit that they too might be annihilated in case of a nuclear conflict, but the Soviet Union and the United States are aware of the terrible consequences a nuclear conflict might have. In the past, planners for peace have vied with planners for war in the councils of state. In our time peace has become a necessity and nuclear war a possibility which we can not contemplate.

The new constellation of forces provoked by the technological and scientific revolution in the nuclear age obliges nations and peoples to cooperate with each other, in order to prevent large-scale war. As a result, the international community has devised mechanisms for the solution of conflicts and the prevention of war. The United Nations Charter provides for a collective security system. Although the peacekeeping function of the United Nations has not been effective in some areas such as Hungary, the world organization has played a major role in separating potential and real combatants and mediating their differences. Various crisis situations have been assuaged by the efforts of United Na-

---

[36] For example, Kashmir, Lebanon, the Congo, and more recently Cyprus.

tions diplomats.[36] While the League of Nations system was regarded by many states as an alternative to independent national policy, the United Nations peacekeeping function is generally regarded as essential for the preservation of world peace, despite the fact that the major powers have not always seen fit to use it. It is conceivable, of course, that the United Nations may lose in political effectiveness as a result of an imbalance of forces in the General Assembly: one, a permanent voting superiority of smaller or less powerful states over major nuclear powers could lead to a diminution of the importance of the United Nations in the long run; two, on the other hand, if the less developed nations are not adequately represented on the various U.N. organs, dissension will result; three, the inability of the underdeveloped nations to clarify and agree on their own areas of interest may become a real source of conflict. Nevertheless, the interdependence of nations and peoples which has been recognized implicitly in the resort of states to collective diplomacy remains a fact of international life. The balancing of forces in the international sphere has become as much a task for international government as the resolution of differences between individuals and groups in any nation.

International conciliation, arbitration, mediation, and good offices are prerequisites for a world order. The function of international organization like the function of government in the state, is to assist peoples, i.e. the individuals who make up a people, in their quest for happiness. In the nationstate, groups may decide to adopt a more or less authoritarian structure; they are restrained, however, if they attempt to impose their authoritarianism on others. Similarly, in the international community states may follow a more or less government-controlled pattern; they must be checked, however, if they try to impose their conceptions of government on others who oppose them.

It has been said that authoritarianism contains the seeds

of violent action. How then is it possible to prevent coercive actions by authoritarian communities in the international sphere? If it becomes necessary for government to restrain by force those elements in society which insist on interfering with the freedom of groups or individuals with whom they disagree, the same would hold true in the international sphere. As peace is a dynamic, progressive state of affairs which requires on the one hand, cultivation of effective means for the solution of conflict, and on the other, active prevention of aggression and punishment of aggressors, so also a peaceful international community must provide mechanisms for the solution of outstanding problems and for restraining aggressors.

Modern international law provides for international organization to help the nations and peoples of the world solve their problems, and international criminal law fulfills the same purpose as the restraining criminal law of any state. The double-edged sword of freedom and the double-edged conception of peace, namely the positive function in terms of services and the protective function in terms of safeguards of liberty, must both be realized to the fullest possible extent, if the aggressive tendencies of authoritarian communities just as aggressive tendencies of individuals or groups in a state are to be checked. The United Nations and its specialized agencies already provide organizations like the UNEF now operating in Cyprus, that maintain a network of services which encompass to some extent both functions. The most pressing economic and social problems are met to an increasing degree by international organizations, and to some extent military necessities are also fulfilled in certain areas.[37]

It might be objected that the United Nations is not a world government, but merely a council of nations. Interna-

---

[37] It should be noted that as the twentieth session of the General Assembly began eleven nations had earmarked national forces for international use.

tional law and international organization recognize the primary importance of the individual. According to the United Nations Charter, violations of human rights or basic provisions of the Charter can not be excused on grounds that they take place within the national sovereignty of any state. Article II, Section 7 of the Charter provides that the United Nations may not interfere in the internal affairs of any country, except in case of enforcement action which may have been prompted by violations of basic principles of international law.

While the United Nations is not at this time a superstate or a world government, it can act to resolve conflicts in the world, if a majority of states approves. This does not mean that an automatic majority in the United Nations is necessarily synonymous with international law. But as long as the United Nations is accepted in its present form and with its present responsibilities by most states, endorsement by the majority of members can be regarded as tangible evidence of international law. The main restriction on the functions of the United Nations as with the functions of any governmental authority is that interference with the freedom of individuals and groups in the world must be justified in terms of necessity. Generally speaking, individuals and groups must be left free to work out their destinies. But an infringement on human rights or a violation of the independence of any group or individual by a state can not be regarded as a purely "domestic affair;" such conflict situations whether they occur in a state or as a result of differences between states can become of international concern,— see, for example, the policy of the U.N. in the past with regard to the future of colonial peoples, and more recently toward the Republic of South Africa and the Congo. They may, therefore, fall within the jurisdiction of the international community acting through the United Nations or any other such organization.

Finally, it is necessary to consider the argument that international differences have often been solved outside of international organizations, namely through bilateral or multilateral negotiations. It is clear that resort to international agencies is not mandatory. International organization like national government is only a mechanism. If conflict situations can be resolved through direct negotiations between nations, then this might even be preferable to an international debate. The United Nations has at times encouraged direct negotiations among nations. According to the philosophy of freedom, the important thing is to realize that international peace depends on the enforcement of the standards of freedom, which means respect for differences as well as cooperation where it is necessary. Interdependence has become a fact of international life; it should teach all peoples the need for cooperation in this sense.

Power for Peace and the Struggle for Freedom

Resolution of differences between states sometimes requires the use of force. According to international law, force may be resorted to under the following conditions: one, in exercise of the right of self-defense (Article 51 of the United Nations Charter); two, in fulfillment of an international mandate (Chapter 7 of the U.N. Charter); and three, to deal with any "threat to the peace, breach of the peace, or act of aggression" not involving armed attack, if the United Nations is unable to act and there is an instant and overwhelming need for such action (Article 2/2 in conjunction with Articles 11 and 39 of the Charter). States, therefore, have the right to resort to force under certain circumstances. They may not, however, have recourse to force as an instrument of national policy; the pursuit of such action was formally denounced in the Kellogg-Briand Pact, the Charter of the United Nations, and the Judgment of Nuremberg.

Of the three reasons cited for waging war, the third is controversial; certain international lawyers maintain that force may only be used in self-defense or in fulfillment of an international mandate. The third reason is just as important, however, because it involves the basic question of the effectiveness of the United Nations in dealing with problems that constitute real or potential threats to international peace. It is clear that if the world organization is unable to solve such problems in time, states may find it necessary to use force, in order to remove grave and imminent threats to their security. In this sense Oliver Wendell Holmes' standard of "clear and present danger" holds true for the international sphere as it does in the nation.

Unfortunately, aggressive elements in the international community still resort to war and warlike means for the achievement of their objectives. The Soviet invasion of Hungary, the aggression of North Korea against South Korea, the Chinese invasion of India, the current struggle in Vietnam, and other such incidents show that war has by no means become obsolete. The major problem for statesmen remains the achievement of peace and the prevention of aggression. As they have been developed in any civilized state, effective means must now be devised on the international level to control armed conflict.

There is basically no limit to the jurisdiction the international community can assume, to the actions it can take (through the United Nations or regional organizations), to the measures it can pursue (from sanction and censure to arbitration and mediation) to counter real or potential threats to the peace. Proceedings either unilateral or multilateral undertaken in this "twilight" zone should be guided by the yardsticks of proportionality to the cause and by effectiveness of the action taken to secure relief. Nations should pressure disputants to use the machinery available, for the pacific settlement of disputes. This would not preclude, however, the institution of remedies without their consent where problems of international peace and security are involved.

Since 1945 three types of security actions have evolved: one, international action as it took place in Korea; two, co-operative action as it is taking place in Vietnam; and three, unilateral action like the action of Israel against the Arab *fedayen*. All such actions are subject to judgment. In the United Nations, Red China was branded an aggressor; at the Nuremberg trials statesmen were condemned for resorting to force in violation of principles of international law. Thus both states and individuals may be held accountable. The absence of a judgment does not necessarily imply approval; the fact that the United Nations acquiesced in the U.S. action against Cuba during the missile crisis means that the matter was "settled out of court." The resort to force always involves a calculated risk.

The defense of peace requires power; if the United States and other member nations of the U.N. who participated in the police action in Korea had not had sufficient military strength, South Korea would have been overrun by the armies of North Korea and the aggression would have succeeded. It is necessary, therefore, to possess military arsenals either collectively or individually, in order to check real or potential aggression. This does not mean that large-scale disarmament is not possible. So long as any nation possesses weapons with which it can threaten other nations, however, a certain balance of power, or as Winston Churchill called it "balance of terror," is inevitable. The challenge for statesmen in a world threatened by nuclear war is to provide a certain degree of military security against possible attacks and at the same time, to work toward a gradual reduction of the military threat through arms control and disarmament. Security and arms control complement each other; one decreases as the other increases, and one becomes less and less necessary as the other succeeds.

Does this mean that the world can exist without any arms

whatsoever? As Hannah Arendt has pointed out in her work on revolution, insurgencies may be the alternative to war in the world of tomorrow. As long as human nature is what it is, a mixture of aggressive and passive impulses, it will be necessary to maintain certain control authorities. An international police force would be the logical substitute for national armies or collective security arrangements like NATO and the Warsaw Pact. Before, however, a truly international police force becomes possible, it will be necessary to provide mechanisms for the resolution of international conflict. These mechanisms may be legal or political in nature; Article 33 of the U.N. Charter lists a number of ways in which disputes can be settled, such as negotiation, enquiry, mediation, conciliation, arbitration, judicial settlement, resort to regional agencies, etc. As the differences between nations become less acute, it should be possible to work out further arms control agreements. In the event of comprehensive disarmament arrangements, an international policing authority would arise as a matter of course. It might be organized under the auspices of the United Nations or on a multilateral basis.

The ecumenical spirit of the Catholic Church today indicates that diversity can exist within unity. The Church which once waged war against heretics and dissenters now proclaims the brotherhood of all men regardless of their faiths. Similarly, the Nuclear Test Ban Treaty indicates that the Soviet Union is able to cooperate with the United States and other countries in the achievement of arms control agreements. Hopefully, this may be a sign of developing erosion of communist authoritarianism. Economic decentralization in Russia as advocated by the Soviet economist Lieberman is another indication of the "thaw."

The struggle for freedom entails diplomacy on many fronts: on the one hand, it is necessary to maintain forces in defense of the free countries; on the other, it is necessary for

the free nations to reach out to peoples of good will everywhere and to create an ideological front against authoritarianism throughout the world. The problem of defense must
be seen positively according to the philosophy of freedom;
neither a "containment" nor a "liberation" policy is feasible
in an age of nuclear war. Only the collective efforts of individuals on all sides of the iron and bamboo curtains to
advance freedom piecemeal step by step, according to circumstances, can insure truly heartfelt responses on the part
of the peoples of the world. Power must not be seen in terms
of national policy and interest as far as the struggle for freedom is concerned. If power is used to advance aggressive
national interests, it can not be rationalized as a defense of
freedom, even if it is incidentally, a protection for a democracy. Such power diplomacy is nothing but imperialism since
it imposes dominion on peoples without their consent, and
if pursued by democracies, represents a perversion of democratic ideals.

According to modern international law, the statement "My
country right or wrong" is not viable; individuals who aid
and abet a national war effort which is contrary to international law may now be made personally responsible for
"crimes against peace." The struggle for freedom and the
pooling of the resources of free peoples everywhere in advancement of the ideals of liberty is not essentially a nation-
alistic endeavor, even if nations are the mechanisms for collective cooperation. Such a struggle must be seen in terms of
the rights of individuals which are threatened wherever and
whenever aggression occurs.

Power for peace can then be considered insurance against
aggression. With the vision of freedom rather than national
interest as the goal of military defense and action, whenever
it becomes unavoidable, exploitation of one country by another becomes less possible both for aggressors and defenders who might be tempted by new-found power as a re-

sult of victory or occupation.

This discussion should not in any way be construed as a sanction for the resort to arms as means for the resolution of conflict. Even if an act of aggression has occurred, it may be advisable to attempt a settlement of differences by peaceful means. Military conquest can not solve the deeper underlying differences between peoples and nations. These may be postponed or delayed or suppressed; but they are not removed by military means. The main objective, therefore, of military planning for peace like any other kind of planning must be the correlation of efforts to promote the happiness of individuals.

The matching of an aggressor with armed force may be unavoidable; but persuasion on the long run must take other forms, such as political cooperation, economic aid, cultural and educational exchange, etc. Power for peace, according to the philosophy of freedom, means power to back up peaceful negotiations for the settlement of international differences. This is in contrast to the policy of authoritarian states which make use of war as a means to an end. Finally, war is reprehensible for freedom-loving persons, because it degrades human dignity and curtails freedom of action. Human dignity is at a loss as a result of the bloodshed and destruction wrought by war. The struggle for freedom involves as much the abolition of war, therefore, as it does the removal of other causes of disharmony in human society.

6

CULTURAL AND SPIRITUAL VALUES IN A FREE SOCIETY

The Problem of Work and the Problem of Leisure

Most political theorists stipulate the good life as the aim of their calculations. Work is only a means toward that end. Karl Marx was poetic, when he described the benefits of the good life: the day when people would be able to fish and enjoy leisure instead of working long hours for the benefit of the ruling classes. Plato envisioned the happiness of a well-integrated citizenry in his ideal state: Aristotle described the virtue of the golden mean; and Rousseau rhapsodized about the natural life. Political planners invariably try to impress their followers with the grandeur of their vision. Thus they are able to demand sacrifices for the sake of future rewards. The people have followed in the expectation of a better, happier existence. And too often, as history shows, they are disappointed.

In modern times science and technology promise a better life. Each century has a particular theme: in the eighteenth century it was enlightenment; in the nineteenth perhaps romanticism and idealism; and in the twentieth century it is the vision of a secure world benefiting from the fruits of scientific achievement. The technological revolution initiated by the atomic age has brought with it automation, shorter working hours, and the possibility of abolishing various kinds of labor. Machines now do what human beings used to do; it is conceivable that this revolution will supplant human labor in most industries. The vision of a society in which robots and automatons and computers will be discharging functions which would have been difficult for human beings to do in the past, can be a pleasing one to contemplate.

Leisure time, however, poses its own special problems. It may become as conformistic as work and constitute a threat to individuality. For example, people may be harnessed into a series of Butlin holiday camps, without, of course, implying that such enjoyment is necessarily base or frivolous. The problem is that many may not be able to develop their gifts and talents to the maximum of their ability, if they are not acquainted with ways and means of using their leisure time.

It has been suggested that education do the job that labor used to do in training people. Leisure would become an educational process for the "making of men" in the new society. Instead of people learning skills of work, they would be taught skills for use in their free time. They may be taught how to paint, write, enjoy and play musical instruments, or work with their hands.

Is it possible to say that people will necessarily submit to this educational process and can one assume that they will be satisfied after being taught basic leisure skills? Will they not perhaps submit to as much of a conformity of leisure as they conformed to conditions of work? This is not to cast doubt on the abilities of people to solve their own problems; but an exaggerated belief in the capacity of persons to adjust to new conditions could produce even greater problems. A society which places a high value on the ideal of leisure and the supplanting of labor may also be responsible for stagnation of mind and spirit. Man has always required incentives to move his imagination. Even if the visions that he has followed from time to time have been false and have perhaps wrought havoc, the human quest must be understood in terms of these hopes. It is necessary to find a realistic way of bridging the mixed leisure-work society in which we live today toward a world in which individuals will be able to use their time for the most constructive, individualistic, humane purposes.

If man appreciates security and entertainment, i.e. passive entertainment, above all other values, then it is unlikely that he will bother to produce special contributions in the various fields of human endeavor, such as art, music, drama, etc. The prospect of an affluent humanity sitting before super-television screens broadcasting programs from space does not inspire much confidence in individual creativity. It might be objected that man's happiness is not measured in terms of creativity. Creativity as described above may be seen as an elite ideal rather than as a value for the majority. It should, however, be remembered that creative individuals often discover the opportunity for their self-expression and self-fulfillment after they have been offered sufficient incentives. Such individuals are carefully nurtured, cultivated by their parents or in school, or by persons whom they respect. It is not possible to rely on the instincts of man under any conditions, even the most affluent ones, in order to help human beings toward the fullest realization of their potential.

The history of the arts and sciences shows that man can find great satisfaction in the achievement of artistic, cultural goals. It would seem, therefore, that part of the function of the state would be to encourage cultural pursuits among the populace. In this way individuals would be assisted in the development of their potential. Against this proposition it might be argued that state encouragement and the allotment of subsidies would produce the kind of conformity that can be so devastating to creative freedom. This criticism might indeed by valid, if the state or other mechanisms of society attempted to impose one standard on individuals.

Competition between different standards is the best way of insuring the finest product. Consequently, encouragement to artists and the populace in general must be free from constraint. Rather, such encouragement should take the form of incentives to unimpeded self-expression.

The economically-minded in our body politic may object that encouragement to fantastic, esoteric, artistic designs or experiments would be a waste. The prize-winning short film *A Bowl of Cherries*, for example, showed that the slapping of paint on canvas by the untalented would be difficult to justify in terms of standards. In a free society the state is not obliged to assist all esoteric pursuits; the point is that it must not interfere with them. Subsidization of artistic, cultural efforts must be subject to some control by the body politic; but the most extreme, individualistic creations can not and should not be suppressed, unless, of course, they are thought to constitute a direct provocation and threat to the public order, which would be difficult to substantiate. Censorship in a free society must be carefully circumscribed. The essence of artistic and cultural freedom lies in the encouragement of all pursuits without necessarily implying approval.

Certain philosophers, Plato, for example, found it difficult to justify the existence of the artist in the ideal state. Their vision was primarily a political and perfectionist one. In Nazi Germany cultural pursuits were at an all time ebb among a people known for outstanding cultural accomplishments. It would, however, be wrong to conclude that authoritarian or dictatorial controls always suppress artistic creativeness; the rule of the Medicis was most encouraging to such artists as Michelangelo. But it is nevertheless true that individualistic art has been impeded by conformistic, authoritarian standards. In past ages it was possible for the creative person to emigrate to another country; today, however, the world has become too small and methods of control too severe and thorough, and as a result, many artists and members of the intelligentsia have been constrained. The suppression of Boris Pasternak is a recent example. The alternative provided by the philosophy of freedom is the only possible solution for such abuses.

Incentives for Cultural and Spiritual
Growth in a Free Society

Incentives may be monetary, but they may also be cultural, social, and spiritual. In the American society financial. incentives have always played a major role in stimulating economic growth and development. Money became for many persons the highest standard of value, since it could carry both economic and social prestige. It would be wrong to conclude from this, however, that money has been the only standard of value in the United States. Since the beginning of the nation there have been people in this country who have valued cultural incentives and spiritual ideals higher than money. The lives of innumerable American artists and musicians as well as the activities of American missionaries at home and abroad support this observation; names such as Homer, Sargent, MacDowell, Copeland, and Dooley come quickly to mind. In fact, the dedication of these individuals and the influence they have commanded in the eyes of other Americans would seem to indicate that cultural and spiritual incentives can be greatly rewarding in human terms.

In the Soviet Union material incentives have largely taken the place of the idealistic "partmaximum" standards of the early revolutionary period.[38] The Marxist norm "to give according to need and to take according to ability" has become "to give according to contribution, and to take according to ability." The system of incentives has been taken to extreme lengths. It begins in the school and extends to

---

[38] J. V. Stalin, *Works*, (Russ.), Vol. 13, pp. 55 *et seq.* Statement on the introduction of the accord system, June 23, 1931.

all branches of professional life. Has this arrangement been conducive to progress in Soviet society? The answer to this question depends on the kind of progress referred to.

In the economic sphere, incentives have proved reasonably successful in stimulating initiative. They were not sufficient by themselves, however, and the Soviet leadership had to institute control authorities, in order to guarantee standards. Persons who did not live up to the "plan" were punished for their failures. In the cultural sphere, material incentives have made life easier for Soviet artists and musicians than it was under the Czars. Furthermore, they have increased interest on the part of many young Soviet citizens in these pursuits. This would only account for a larger number of artists and musicians, however, and does not necessarily mean that the standards of performance are higher in that society as compared to others where material incentives are lower. Shostakovich, Khachaturian, and Prokofiev are geniuses who would probably have made their mark under any circumstances. It might be more correct to conclude, therefore, that cultural growth depends on cultural incentives. The prestige status attached to cultural endeavors in Soviet society may be more responsible for the development of the creative arts there today than material incentives.

Spiritual incentives have for centuries influenced people to devote long hours to prayer and meditation. Psychologists might argue that such motivations are psychological rather than spiritual. This would be true for any incentives, however. The fact that some individuals are more responsive to spiritual incentives than to cultural or material incentives does not mean that one or the other is spurious. The intensity of dedication, however, on the part of individuals pursuing spiritual incentives is usually greater than those serving material gain. Spiritual growth in a society has accounted for a deeper awareness of the meaning of life. Disappointments and setbacks which to the materialist must seem like standards of failure become modes of destiny to those who seek satisfaction in a highly personal, inner life.

The growing insecurity among many people today would seem to indicate that spiritual incentives are not as powerful as they once were. Nevertheless, the success achieved by Pope John XXIII in appealing to the deeper human instincts of people everywhere shows that spiritual incentives are not dead. In the Soviet Union spiritual incentives are discouraged; the philosophy of communism regards Christian spiritual incentives as dangerous to the authority of the state. In Russia the Marxist precept that "religion is the opiate of the people" led to widespread persecution of the religious. While the Soviet Constitution guarantees freedom of worship as well as freedom of anti-religious propaganda (Article 124), religious pursuits are frowned on by the authorities and the religious-minded are excluded from important positions in Soviet society. Nevertheless, in Soviet Russia today millions continue to practice the faith of their ancestors.

In the free societies religion is not regarded with disfavor. In Western Europe, the United States, in Arab and some Asian countries, religion is not only tolerated, but approved of. While there are millions of agnostics and atheists in the world today, the influence of religion persists.

Cultural and spiritual incentives are necessary for the fullest development of man's potential. What form they take is another matter; in a free society this is a subject for individual conscience. If matter is regarded as the total substance of existence in the universe, then spirit is immanent in matter. The late Teilhard de Chardin, scientist and philosopher, thought that spirit is infused into all things.[39] Perhaps materialists will eventually realize that the spiritual quest is as much part of their natures as the spiritualists seem to have realized that matter is not evil, but part of the spiritual

---

[39] Pierre Teilhard de Chardin, *The Divine Milieu,* New York: Harper & Brothers, 1960. See also his *Phenomenon of Man.*

realm.

Whatever the outcome of these speculations, different kinds of incentives should be allowed to compete with each other for acceptance. Neither material nor spiritual nor cultural incentives should be imposed on anyone; but each individual should try to find his happiness and his standards, i.e. his own incentives. The denial of such rights to persons can only lead to a diminution of their human potential. Individuals who cut themselves off from the world or who categorically deny the validity of others' standards impose on themselves a kind of tyranny which narrows and confines their personalities. The challenge must be, therefore, to stimulate people with different kinds of incentives so that they may find the way which suits them best.[40]

Spirit Versus Law in the Ideal State

The accusation that a too free society breeds anarchy has been discussed. However, the problem of improving social mechanisms and achieving the common good in the light of the anarchistic tendencies of individuals needs separate consideration. Extreme, libertine behavior threatens the common good and undermines the welfare of the individual. There are some who do not realize that their rights entail obligations. This leads to the question of how such individualistic extremism can be prevented in a free society which recognizes the primacy of the individual?

Law and order are indispensable for the successful functioning of a society. This does not mean, however, that law and regulation are the most effective means for dealing with social disorders. Persuasion which is not codified may be a more effective method for solving social problems. Persuasion which requires force, i.e. compulsion, is always a lesser good, since it deprives someone of his freedom.

In the final analysis, no amount of law or regulation can

---

[40] "Jeder kann nach seiner eigenen Façon selig werden." Frederick the Great.

change the deepest responses of individuals. Law which contradicts the conscience of men is usually violated just as law which does not take into consideration general behavior patterns. Government institutions, law, and even norms of justice can not be a substitute for the innermost struggles and decisions of men. When Rousseau maintained that the individual could be reconciled with the state through law, he overlooked the fact that individuals are quite different from each other.[41] Law as it is usually understood, is a social regulator and not an individualistic creation. The need for general law is understood; but this does not in any way change the basic human requirement for individual standards. Even if these standards are derived socially, that is, from environment and heredity, there is still the individual initiative and response. Regardless of the many mechanisms, pressure groups, or family connections to which man owes allegiance, in his heart he remains always a unique entity.

There is no unbridgeable gap between the social kind of law or community law and personal standards if a person is well-integrated in society. Usually the social authority blames an individual for not adjusting sufficiently, if he is found wanting in his conformity. Some behaviorists have also blamed the social situation for its effects on individuals. It is useless to speculate on responsibility in this fashion, because persons are both private and social. In this double function they partake of different realms of experience. The personal realm can be described as spiritual, especially if it has religious content; the social realm is communal.

The state and the individual are reconciled not through law, but through a concern of individuals for each other's needs, a concern expressed directly or indirectly through mechanisms of government. Thus the whole fabric of the

---

[41] "The laws are properly but the conditions of civil association. The people submit themselves to the laws, and ought to enjoy the right of making them; it pertains only to those who associate to regulate the terms of the society." See Rousseau, *op. cit.*, Chap. VI for discussion of this point.

state becomes nothing more or less than a means for men to help each other fulfill themselves. The emphasis is not on any abstract common good, but on the very real needs of each individual member of the body politic.

In a mass society a man's voice is stifled and his individuality suppressed when the mechanisms of control, governmental and non-governmental, become so overwhelming that he feels any expression of preference would be practically futile. His sense of efficacy as a citizen is lost amidst conflicting interests. It is to solve this dilemma, to help individuals communicate more effectively, to bring about a constant dialogue between government and the governed that the philosophy of freedom begins with those rights basic to the individual.

In past ages the church would claim a special prerogative in helping individuals solve their personal problems. The churches, however, have not been so successful, as the history of world religion indicates. Nevertheless, some progress has been made since the days of the Crusades. There are, however, still those who would launch all kinds of crusades at the expense of people's lives and happiness, if given the opportunity. The philosophy described here is no substitute for pacifist desires; it is strong in the defense of rights and its conclusions are based on the needs of individuals and their legitimate concern with power. The framework thus provided allows for the fullest expression of man's spirit when directed towards his personal fulfillment and the good of his neighbor. When law is compatible with the spirit of man, it becomes the cornerstone of a free society.

Freedom

In The

Modern State

7

FREEDOM IN A DEMOCRATIC STATE

Characteristics of Democracy

The philosophy of freedom should be implemented through a system of government adapted to the prevailing conditions. The philosophy is not associated with any particular form of government; but some forms of government are more conducive to its fulfillment than others. The first form to be examined in this regard is democracy.

Democracy literally translated, means rule of the people. In practice, however, it is not the unqualified power of the mob; it is rather government for all the people, which means for the interests of every individual member of the body politic. As defined above, it would seem that democracy is the best mechanism for the implementation of the philosophy of freedom. This need not be so, however, because the mechanisms for control in a democracy may be inadequate to the task set out by the philosophy of freedom. If the mechanisms of state are designed to protect the interests of a few, or if they lead to the tyranny of the majority, they are not conducive to the needs of the people. The point is that mechanisms of democracy must be suited to the fulfillment of the aims of freedom just like mechanisms of any other form of government should serve the ideals which are considered most important for the welfare of the populace.

There are different kinds of democracy; the most important types known today are presidential democracy and parliamentary democracy. Presidential democracy as it exists in the United States, is a complicated system of separation of powers, i.e. executive, legislative, and judicial, combined with checks and balances, within a federal framework. The essence of American democracy is rule of the majority checked by procedural safeguards. The Bill of Rights of the American Constitution represents a substantive limitation on the functions of government. But most important in the workings of the American democracy is not the conception of individual rights, but procedures or mechanisms which will prevent arbitrary exercises of power.

In modern times, however, the service function of government has become as important as protection. The New Deal and Fair Deal of Franklin Roosevelt and Harry Truman provided the country with complicated machinery for serving the people's needs. Problems have arisen time and again in the workings of the modern American democracy regarding the balance of protection versus achievement. Robert Hutchins refers to this anti-thesis of values in his *Two Faces of Federalism*.[42] Actually, the anti-thesis has been somewhat resolved in practice. According to the practitioners of American democracy, the President, Congress, and the Supreme Court, the rights of the people include a right to service. American democracy is, therefore, an amalgam of popular institutions, bureaucracy, constitutional and extra-constitutional mechanisms, which serve to fulfill people's needs by providing services and protection.

Parliamentary democracy as it is practiced in England, allows for more direct rule by the representatives of the people. Checks and balances are not as developed in most parliamentary democracies as they are in the United States. The British democracy has survived as the oldest democracy in world history, because the Bill of Rights, constitutional safeguards, the conceptions of limited government, freedom of dissent, etc. have become part of the consciousness of the

---

[42] Robert M. Hutchins, *Two Faces of Federalism*, Santa Barbara, Calif.: Center for the Study of Democratic Institutions, 1961, p. 22.

British people. This perhaps explains why checks and balances are not as necessary for the safeguarding of individual rights in England as they might be in the United States. De Tocqueville spoke of the tyranny of the majority in America; the imposition of such majority or mob rule in England today is almost inconceivable. The genius of the British system lies in the awareness of the British people of the necessity to safeguard human rights generally. If this awareness were less developed, it is possible that the English might have yielded to periodic reactions toward authoritarianism as Americans experienced during the McCarthy period. The British example proves that, in the final analysis, no philosophy or framework of government is a substitute for the wills, intentions, desires and hopes of individuals. Winston Churchill and his brave opposition to the forces of fascism during the Second World War is a prime example of the undaunted, defiant spirit of individualism which has so long guarded and advanced the ideals of British democracy. In our time this example has received additional confirmation in the unusual feat of British diplomacy which transformed an empire into a commonwealth and thereby prevented bloodshed and rebellion.

The main characteristics of both presidential and parliamentary democracy are indirect rule of the people, delegation of power through representatives, checks and balances, extra-constitutional mechanisms for the implementation of individual choices, e.g. parties, pressure groups, etc., and generally, a consciousness of the value of individual freedom. The shortcomings of both the British and American systems are a certain lack of response on the part of many people to particular challenges, such as Hitler's invasion of the Rhineland, and an occasional paralysis of government in times of crisis coupled with a certain inability of the people to control their leaders during such periods. The inability of the people to control the actions of a particular leader like Anthony Eden during the Suez crisis is perhaps the most serious flaw in modern democracy. It poses a real challenge in terms of the survival of freedom. The lack of communication between the people and their representatives is probably the main cause of this condition.

The question that the modern example or examples of presidential and parliamentary democracy pose is whether modern needs have become too complex, too distant for the majority of citizens to understand. Does this query apply to the workings of the state? Could it be that the Platonic example of an ideal government guided by experts is more appropriate today than institutions founded during a more primitive, agricultural stage of development? According to the philosophy described here, there is no substitute for the wishes of an individual. No computer, no expert, no specialist can take his place. The problem is how to enable him to control the experts, computers, etc., and to make more meaningful choices. Education is an important means toward that end; but it is not the only one. The liberation of the human spirit from various social pressures may be even more conducive to the fulfillment of an individual's potential, especially if the restrictions imposed are not justified in terms of need.

Protection Versus Achievement

The essence of the democratic state is the dispersion of power; the aim is to provide different points of decision-making so that the individual has maximum freedom in appealing to different authorities for justice. Thus, the danger of monolithic government and dictatorship is avoided. One result of this system has, however, been a certain paralysis between different branches of government. Protection of the citizen is not the only function of government. Services which require a high degree of coordination are impeded by excessive checks and balances which hamstring the practical efforts of government. The executive is prevented from fulfilling its mandate by an excessively zealous legislature, and the judiciary can nullify the efforts of the legislature and executive through judicial review.

Another force which might prevent action is public opinion. The apathy of the British populace in the thirties might account for the unrealistic policies of Prime Minister Chamberlain whose appeasement of Hitler did not prevent the outbreak of World War II. On the contrary, a more aggressive policy as recommended by Churchill, but which was unpopular with the majority at the time, might have been more effective.

The difficulties facing a democratic mechanism are compounded in the underdeveloped or less industrialized countries of Asia and Africa. Federalism in India has not been as successful as originally imagined; the revolt in Kerala brought intervention by the central government. Strong men like Nkrumah in Ghana and Sukarno in Indonesia, for example, have surmised that democracy has to be guided. They believe that strong leadership is the most effective way of dealing with the pressing problems of industrialization and modernization facing their countries today. This approach, however, often leads to dictatorship.

The question that must be asked is whether achievement or the attainment of high standards of living, i.e., the solution to pressing problems of economic need and social imbalance, requires strong government while extreme individualism tends to undermine the necessary authority of government. Has protection become less important in our time? The achievement of decent living standards is as much a realization of a basic human right as the protection of freedoms guaranteed in the Bill of Rights. The right to survive, or freedom from want, is a basic concern to all human beings. It is false to separate economic survival as a right from other rights like freedom of speech, freedom of press, etc. There is no dichotomy then between efforts to achieve higher living standards, in order to solve basic problems of human need in the economic and social spheres and the protection of traditional liberties as they are anchored in the Bill of Rights. The human being must be treated as a whole; his physical being is as much a part of him as his mental or his spiritual faculties.

Does this mean, however, that one right or another takes precedence? This is a question of priorities that has to be settled in accordance with standards of law and justice; the mechanisms for settling such questions are of crucial importance in the day to day working of a democracy. As now devised in parliamentarian and presidential democracies, are they adequate for our current needs? Or does the occasional paralysis which results from checks and balances impede progress unnecessarily? As previously noted, checks and balances, the separation of powers, federalism, and other mechanisms designed to guarantee a wide dispersion of powers, are in effect, ways and means to restrict government authority for the sake of greater individual liberty; and these restrictions on government authority might have to be abrogated or limited in cases of need. Restrictions on liberty only in proportion to necessity is the standard which should guide the policymaker in applying a mechanism designed to fulfill human dignity. If necessity requires restriction on certain liberties, in order to allow individuals to survive, then the governmental mechanisms must be adjusted to these ends. The problem is who will determine the occasion for necessity and how a decision with regard to such a matter should be translated into action.

It would be simple to conclude that the people in a democracy by definition have the right to decide when necessity compels a restriction on their liberties. The answer, however, is more complex; obviously, the people may not be in possession of all the facts, and they may not be ready for any drastic change which is necessary for their welfare. Does this mean that experts must take over by default? Theoretically, no denial of a people's rights can be justified except in terms of greater individual freedom of choice. Individuals in a body politic delegate responsibilities to their representatives. If in interaction with each other, different branches of government, that is popular institutions, the executive, legislature, etc., heed a consensus or near consensus which sanctions certain restrictions on liberties and innovations for the common good, then it is impossible to speak of government by fiat. In such an event, the decision as to priorities of rights, i.e. necessities, will have been made through the ordinary workings of the democratic process.

But what if the governmental organization, pressure groups and political parties, etc., are inadequate to this task, if they do not reflect popular choices and are unable to cope with a crisis? What if a strong man seizes power? In some countries strong leadership is the only hope for the maintenance of some degree of law and order. But if a dictator seizes power, it is impossible to speak of democracy any longer; the people's choices will have been subsumed by the action of their leaders. The maintenance of freedom depends on the voluntary efforts and cooperation of the individual members of the body politic, and if the people fail in their responsibilities, the end result may be another form of government which no longer has anything to do with democracy.

While people may not be sufficiently qualified to judge all the innovations necessary for the welfare of society, they do have a kind of veto power over the proposals of their leaders. The philosophy of freedom provides that government can institute services as long as these do not violate basic liberties. The people have a right to veto services and innovations, but this does not preclude the initiative of leaders who realize the need for change. The interaction between dynamic leadership and watchful citizenry is the best hope for the survival of democracy in our time. This is as true for the less industrialized countries as it is for the more advanced democracies. The manifestations of popular choices in the developing countries may be more drastic or flagrant, in view of the more pressing needs; but essentially the process is the same: people indicate their choices and the leaders suggest necessary changes and *vice versa*. In this way the protection of individual rights and the need for achievement are reconciled. The fulfillment of rights, i.e. economic, social and other rights, provides the key to the successful functioning of a democratic mechanism.

Democracy and World Affairs

Democracy relies on the voluntary expression of choices by the individual members of the body politic. The electoral process and certain devices such as the initiative, referendum, and recall, are designed to facilitate such choices. In that sense, democracy and the philosophy of freedom are synonymous. The challenge of democracy as an ideology and way of life is to preserve basic rights of choice for all citizens while facilitating in some instances the verdict of the majority. In the final analysis, it is the common good and not the good of a plurality or majority which is essential for the effective functioning of any form of government. Human dignity and human rights demand the protection of individuals regardless of how non-conformist they may be. Majority rule must be tempered by minority rights in a free society.

The responsibilities of a democracy toward the rest of the world poses special problems. For example, does the commitment to human rights, the Bill of Rights, the Declaration of Human Rights, etc. require a pacifist or a militant stand agains violations of basic liberties wherever they may occur? Since 1945 the United States and other Western democracies have been engaged in a battle against communist authoritarianism. The main theme of this struggle has been the preservation of national self-determination for peoples in

Europe, Asia, and Africa, and the advancement of concepts of human rights. The communists claim that these slogans are mere coverups for the exploitation of the poor and less privileged.

As stated earlier, a form of "democratic centralism" is authorized in communist countries. This system turns out usually to be more centralistic than democratic. The alienation of the highest echelons of leadership from the local Soviets as a result of the extreme delegation of powers prevents the fullest exercise of political rights by the mass of the people. The individuals who make up the local communities are generally too distant from the centers of decision-making to influence policy. The sudden change-over from Khrushchev to Kosygin and Brezhnev is an example of the lack of popular control.

It is clear that capitalist economies suffer occasionally from serious contradictions of values of freedom; and it is also clear that communist countries have experienced suppression of individual rights. When individuals suffer from extreme want in the so-called free countries, they can not be said to possess all their rights; this is especially true, if their very livelihood and survival is threatened. Similarly, if individuals are denied basic liberties, such as freedom of speech, press, etc. in the communist countries, they are not enjoying freedom of expression as it has been guaranteed in the Universal Declaration of Human Rights.

Do these contradictions in the capitalist and communist societies blur the lines of responsibility to the extent that neither one side nor the other has the right to maintain or advance conceptions of freedom? Are both the communists and Western democracies hypocritical, when they maintain that they are fighting for freedom? It has been shown that the struggle for freedom entails a global, international approach. Freedom is indivisible. Peoples have a right and an obligation to oppose violations of rights wherever they may occur. In the nation they have the right to overthrow the government, if it becomes a tyranny. In international affairs they have an obligation to protect their less fortunate brethren against tyrannous exercises of power.

Does this mean, however, that nations may interfere in each other's affairs, in order to realize the precepts of the philosophy of freedom as they have been stated? The principle of self-determination like the principle of personal independence is a most important one in the constellation of national of international human rights. Accordingly, if a country has fallen under the sway of a tyrant, is there such a thing as a right to aid revolution?

It can not be said that stagnation or freezing of the *status quo* is a principle of the philosophy of freedom. Freedom is a growing, dynamic process. Forces which would perpetuate conditions that deny basic human rights like freedom from want, freedom from fear, etc. must be considered obstacles to the fullest realization of people's freedom. Does it follow then that the communists are right, when they claim that so-called wars of national liberation should be aided? Can countries and peoples assist other peoples in their wars of liberation?

The United Nations Charter allows for collective self-defense and the execution of international mandates to advance and safeguard the principles of the Charter. Within the framework of international law countries are justified in assisting each other against violators and violations of human rights. The principle of self-determination does not mean that countries may not assist each other under any circumstances. On the contrary, self-determination may involve a large degree of aid, foreign aid, economic assistance, etc., especially in times of crisis. A military emergency or political crisis may also occasion foreign help. The point is not that countries should not assist each other in any crisis; rather, the principle of self-determination provides that such assistance may not take place without the consent of the people involved, barring the circumstance that a country interfered with is an aggressor and branded as such by the international community in accordance with the standards of law.

Are countries free to interpret standards of international law for themselves and to intervene in other countries' affairs, if they deem the law to be on their side? Mechanisms of control are relevant in international law and international relations as they are in national affairs. The United Nations provides a buffer between contending parties. Nations are obliged to resort to peace-making and peace-keeping machinery of the United Nations before they can use force against other states. The only exceptions to this rule are immediate self-defense in case of an overwhelming, grave threat "leaving no time for deliberation" and the rather rare provisions of Articles 107 and 53/2 of the Charter aimed against former Axis states. These latter provisions are the result of World War II alliances against fascism.

The struggle for freedom requires dynamic policies. Peoples may oppose tyrannies that prevent change or which institute exploitative systems of control; but the use of force by one country against another for any cause is carefully circumscribed according to international law. The philosophy of freedom commands respect for the standards of law so long as they are designed to safeguard individuals and peoples against aggression and unwarranted interference. Even if a majority of states in the international community sanctions a particular course, this does not necessarily mean that the policies adopted are legal. The verdict of a majority of states has the *prima facie* evidence of right on its side; but whether or not an action is legal must be subjected to other standards of examination. These are provided in Article 38 of the Statute of the International Court of Justice, i.e. treaties, customs and general principles of law as recognized by civilized states. Basic rights of peoples must be protected even against a majority of states as basic rights of individuals must be maintained against any exercise of tyranny by the majority in a state. Policy in international affairs then is subject to standards of law and justice as government policy is in a state. A law can not be a substitute for the dynamically evolving aims and aspirations of peoples, but it can provide safeguards against extremism.

The international human rights movement is the most dynamic development of our time. The philosophy of freedom has also been referred to as the philosophy of human rights. Democracies in so far as they translate the precepts of the philosophy of freedom into practical mechanisms for the implementation of people's choices have the responsibility to protect and advance the ideals of freedom and human rights in all parts of the world. Although the lines of responsibility are sometimes hazy, and it is not clear whether truth is wholly on one side or another in cases of conflict, this does not absolve people of their obligation to help each other in the struggle for freedom, freedom from want, freedom from oppression, when this struggle is of prime importance for the survival of freedom everywhere. The interdependence of states and peoples demands on the part of the democracies dynamic policies that subscribe to ideals of freedom and facilitate changes more conducive to human dignity. Anti-authoritarianism generally plays a subordinate role in the struggle for freedom. It is perhaps the other side of the coin of battle; but it is not the main content of it. The movement in essence is positive in the sense that it involves constant change and improvement for the achievement of greater freedom.

Democracies or other states which do not assist such changes, but attempt to influence a temporary situation and prevent necessary adjustments to new conditions, are not fulfilling the aims of the philosophy of freedom. They may be anti-communist, or anti-fascist, or whatever, but they are not supporters of freedom. Aiding and abetting dictators and military juntas may be a means toward preventing some greater evil like civil war and extreme chaos; but they can not be an aim unto themselves. Only the active process of building freedom in all spheres for peoples everywhere can be described as the fight for freedom. The attending opposition to anti-free elements in international society is merely a by-product of this primary cause. It is to be hoped that peoples everywhere will come to realize that opposition to conceptions which they do not favor does not mean that they are on the side of the angels.

8

FREEDOM IN A ROMAN REPUBLIC

Leadership in a Roman Republic

The mechanisms of parliamentary and presidential democracies as implemented by certain countries have not proved satisfactory. France, for example, under the Fourth Republic suffered one government crisis after another. As a result, the Fifth Republic limits substantially the powers of the legislature which had previously been the main source of instability. In the American and British democracies, the legislature is of greatest significance in the governing process; in France under General de Gaulle the executive is of primary importance. In view of the growing trend among fledgling democracies for the executive to assume greater powers than originally delegated, it would seem that a kind of Roman Republic might become a more successful form of government than the traditional democracy that we know. A Roman Republic today would combine a high degree of central government power with a senatorial veto right. Perhaps the senatorial voice would not even have the strength of a veto; in any case, democratic or popular control would not be a major objective in the day to day handling of government affairs; rather, the president or chairman of such a republic might submit to an occasional referendum for an opinion on policy as General de Gaulle has done. Is this view of a republic realistic, however, and if so, have the more traditional forms of democracy with their concomitant emphasis on the power of the legislature outlived their usefulness?

For the successful functioning of parliamentary or presidential democracies it is required that on the one hand, the legislature not indulge in extremist tactics to sabotage the government's efforts, and on the other, that the executive not detract from the legitimate powers of the legislature. The ideal stipulated in the separation of powers and checks and balances system, is a high one and one that is extremely difficult to achieve. In the United States and England practical experience shows that usually the most that can be expected is an approximation of the ideal.

In France under the various Republics the pattern is less stable than in England and the United States: either the National Assembly was at times extreme in its insistence on its rights, or the executive suppressed the Assembly. The result was often disruption of the government and civil chaos. Through many government crises the French civil service has governed independently of popular control. This was not necessarily a handicap, since the civil service represented, in some respects, the only stable force in the French governmental process. The Fifth Republic with its greater emphasis on central control is not a new phenomenon in French history; the ambitions of Napoleon III or the programs of the Laval Vichyites during World War II are other examples of strong authoritarian or semi-authoritarian centralized French governments. Does it follow from this that prognostications about a Roman Republic are merely a camouflaged sell-out of representative democracy? Has, in fact, the French Fifth Republic become a form of dictatorship?

The opinions about the strong, central direction given by the present French President are divided on the point whether he has become a dictator in fact, if not in name. The Constitution of the Fifth Republic allows the President to dissolve the National Assembly and to take emergency measures (Article 12). This in itself would not constitute a dic-

tatorial exercise of power; the point is whether these restrictions are justified in terms of greater freedom for the individual or whether they merely represent authoritarian excesses
of power in violation of basic human rights. The French
example is not isolated in our time. Certain less industrialized nations such as Ghana and the United Arab Republic
have found "guided democracy" more suitable to their
needs.

The decline of the power of the legislature and of the
courts in some countries and the growth of power of the
executive are phenomena that seem to be reflected even in
the more traditional forms of democracy. The huge establishment of government in the United States today and the
nationalization programs of Great Britain, for example, show
the growth of centralized power. The services and protection
made available to the people, especially to individuals who
are needy, have liberated many persons from restrictions
due to want, insecurity, illness, etc.

Unfortunately, this development has not been accom-
plished in most countries without some degree of violence.
The experience of France during the last stages of the Alger-
ian Revolution is an example. The growth of central power
in the more traditional democracies has also led to certain
bureaucratic infringements of rights. The American Civil
Liberties Union has been concerned with case after case of
such violations; and the U.S. Supreme Court has repeatedly
dealt with them usually in favor of the individuals involved.
Most dramatic in the United States are the decisions on
search and seizure which curtail the power of the police to
investigate private homes without proper authorization, even
if this gives a certain advantage to the criminals or suspected criminals involved.[43]

On the one hand, it may be concluded that the growth of

---

[43] See for example, *People v. Cahan*, 44 Cal. 2d 434, 445, 282 p. 2d
905, 911-12 (1955).

central power in a Roman Republican system has led to certain benefits for people in terms of security and stability; while one cabinet after another fell in the Fourth Republic, President de Gaulle has been successful in maintaining order. On the other hand, executive power has in many cases led to violations of civil liberties. The problem seems to be how to reconcile the benefits derived from stronger leadership on the part of the executive in countries where the power of the legislature has declined, with adequate safeguards of individual rights.

Freedom-loving leaders whether they be representatives of the people in the legislature or in the executive, fulfill both a trustee and delegate function. As trustees they must act according to their best judgment and conscience in discharging their responsibilities; as delegates they are bound to fulfill the mandate of the people. Since the philosophy of freedom is based on the conception that all government is instituted for the primary aim of assisting individuals in their quest for happiness according to the standards which they choose, the trustee and delegate functions of the leaders in a Roman Republic as in a democracy must be fulfilled with a view to that objective. Leaders may put the trustee function first or they may act according to the mandate they have received depending on the needs, i.e. rights, of the individuals whom they represent. In some instances it may be necessary for the government to exercise greater control than the legislature over the day to day operations of government; but this does not alter the fact that leadership in a free society requires respect for human rights and basic freedoms. How can this objective be safeguarded, however, if an executive or for that matter, a legislature is unwilling to discharge its responsibilities according to these standards?

Checks and balances have been described as an important mechanism for protection of individuals' rights. It is conceivable that in a Roman Republic the courts would be a most important influence in safeguarding individual rights. They might provide a check on the executive on the fulfillment of its program. At the same time, the judicial organs of the state could deal with questions involving civil liberties. Even if the legislature is not strong enough to balance the executive, the judiciary may fulfill a salutary role in achieving the reconciliation between individual freedom and *raison d'état*.

In the final analysis, the different branches of government, i.e. legislature, executive, and judiciary, are responsible to the people. They are means for the fulfillment of the end of greater personal freedom. As means they can never take precedence over direct action by the people. In most societies today pressure groups of one kind or another play an important role in influencing the governmental process. Such pressure groups may be made up of businessmen, labor leaders, journalists, etc. Citizen pressure groups, or consumers' groups, may also constitute checks on governmental authority. Movements of citizens, groups of individuals who take an interest in public affairs. referenda, initiative, recall, etc. may all represent checks to safeguard individual freedom and human rights. Leadership in a Roman Republic must respect certain checks, if it is not to become authoritarian. The test of freedom in a Roman Republic would, therefore, be whether the government tolerates such direct citizen action.

Popular Representation and Popular Rights

A major problem connected with decreasing popular control over government is the increasing responsibility of the bureaucracy. Political theorists and specialists in government are usually occupied with the problem of control of the bureaucracy, their main concern being with the implementation of the directives of the executive. It is clear that a civil service is essential for the effective functioning of government. There is one thing that is overlooked in many of these calculations, however, and that is the role citizens must play in controlling the bureaucracy. The complexities of government may be dealt with by specialists; but there can be no delegation of the final authority of the people.

It is essential, therefore, that individual citizens acquaint themselves with government problems, and to the extent that it is possible, educate themselves in public affairs. If the philosophy of freedom is to be meaningful, the people must exercise their legitimate functions in the area of government. This means that if they are not able to discharge their responsibilities, or are unwilling to do so, any form of government would not be essentially free. Moving on from this point, is it implied that the people have no right to abolish their freedom or to delegate their responsibilities?

Taken to its logical extreme, the philosophy of freedom would have to recognize the right of the people to abolish their freedom. There can be no substitute for the people's choice, or rather the individuals' choice of government, even if this happens to be a dictatorship. If a people choose dictatorship, the result is the destruction of freedom. The two are incompatible.

A Roman Republic would have to guarantee, therefore, the right of people to act directly in influencing government plans and programs, even if the powers of the legislature have been severely curtailed. No branch of government, including the legislature, is sacrosanct. In a Roman Republic as in the more traditional democracies, an essential attribute of a free state and a free society is flexibility. Dispersion of power in a democracy may be an effective way of implementing flexibility. But the system of checks and balances, points of decision-making, may vary from country to country and people to people. The requirements posed by the conditions in any particular country may necessitate different points of decision-making and different checks on governmental authority.

The question that then may be asked is how these checks are to be determined, that is when should a referendum or election be held, and who should decide? In the final analysis, the people themselves must be the judge. Their representatives or leaders may recommend certain solutions, or even try to promulgate them; but the popular choice whether expressed through direct or indirect action must be respected. Otherwise the right to revolution may become an important reference point for popular action. The Declaration of Independence was written after the settlers were unable to gain certain concessions from their British overlords. The right to revolution was the final resort. In our time it has been extended to the international sphere; peoples have a right, if not an obligation, to aid each other in protecting fundamental human rights. In that sense, the transition from colonialism to independence in various countries and the agitation of peoples against antiquated social, economic, and political institutions, is a gigantic revolution for human rights and human dignity.

While it is necessary to regard the different mechanisms of government, be they Roman Republican or traditionally democratic, as means toward an end, this must not in any way be construed as an endorsement. Only if these means are effective in furthering greater freedom of choice for the individual are they fulfilling their function. If they are conducive to authoritarian, dictatorial exercises of power, whether perpetrated by a President, representatives in a legislative committee, or peoples' judges, they must be opposed and the people have the right to abolish them. Those are the words of the Declaration of Independence which apply to our time as they did in 1776.

Planning in a Roman Republic

One of the reputed advantages of "guided democracies" is the possibility for government to plan the orderly progression of economic, social and political processes. A Roman Republic would also enable the leadership to take the initiative in programming necessary changes and innovations, and the Senate or parliament could not hamper the government's efforts as effectively as in more traditional democracies where the legislature is extremely powerful. The decline or diminution of the power of the legislature would not necessarily mean that popular control is lost; in fact, representatives in the legislature can during much of their term act quite independently of their constituents, which means that they may be as removed from popular control in their day to day activity as the executive.

Planning by major political, economic and social forces in a community is essential for progress and while individual initiative is of the greatest importance in stimulating economic and social processes, extreme individualism is a luxury which many countries plagued by want and insecurity can not afford. This is especially true in the less industrialized nations where factionalism not only tends to impede the government's programs, but often leads to violence and bloodshed. The severity of the problems faced by people in these societies appears to create the most intense political reactions. People in Latin America give the impression that political change can solve economic and social problems, when they overthrow one government after another. In the more traditional democracies like the United States and England democratic government is exercised in relative peace. This may be due to the degree of prosperity prevailing in those countries. It might be concluded then that where economic and social problems are most pressing, a greater degree of political control and leadership in planning is required than in those areas where the more advanced stages of economic and social development are quietly underway.

From the standpoint of the philosophy of freedom what

are the most pressing problems confronting countries that have tended toward the example of the Roman Republic? One might argue that pressing economic and social difficulties have been the prime cause of strong leadership and even dictatorship; but this would be a misunderstanding of the relationship between the problems referred to and the processes of government as they have been analyzed in this work. The traditional democracies and free societies in general have been plagued by similar problems without yielding to dictatorial controls beyond short emergency periods. The reason for this is that in these countries conciliation processes have been worked out which are generally effective, and the prevailing consensus supports a resort to such means for the resolution of conflicts. These conciliation processes have in modern times included a high degree of planning. The cause of the trend to dictatorship or a greater degree of authoritarian control in some countries stems in large part, from the lack of conciliation processes. Without a consensus, democratic machinery, if it exists in the first place, breaks down. Organization for planning is essential for the implementation of the philosophy of freedom. The challenge is to make planning an effective means in achieving greater freedom and efficiency in the resolution of problems facing a society.

This would seem to be a commonplace. What then prevents leaders in some countries from devising machinery for the attainment of these objectives? Certain governments may place the ideal of efficiency above all other values. Achievement is regarded as an end unto itself, and as a result, the ideal of freedom may be sacrificed to the ideal of efficiency. As has been pointed out, however, these values are not contradictory; in fact, efficiency in achieving freedom from want, for example, is one means for the achievement of greater freedom. The point is that freedom from want must be considered in connection with other freedoms. An excessive concern for one freedom as opposed to others can be as destructive as an artificial or unconscious distinction between protection and achievement, i.e. freedom and efficiency.

The answer to the problem of authoritarianism posed in connection with the trend to greater central control seems to lie in coordinated planning, that is, planning which connects the different areas of society. This coordination should be a kind of weaving together of the different strands of the elements of freedom. Priorities must be decided in terms of overall balance, and not according to a one-sided or parochial view of human nature and society. An extreme emphasis on the economic, political, or social aspects of a problem to the detriment of freedom in other areas can only lead to an imbalance which may result in conflict. A government that stresses some interests as opposed to others in an extreme fashion, will usually end up being challenged, and its leaders may then resort to drastic means, in order to keep power. An overall balanced view of social problems may require a greater degree of central control in some countries at certain times; but the objective, if framed in terms of freedom, will be a liberating balance of interests rather than an exclusivist control.

Such a balance may well be considered utopian and unattainable. It is clear that if all aspects of a problem are considered in planning, and if leadership is restrained by the multiplicity of interests involved, this may delay planning. It may be necessary for a leadership to act more promptly in an emergency situation. In the final analysis, processes of government are usually pragmatic. Computers and other modern innovations may make them less haphazard and unpredictable; but human decision-making which must rely on innumerable factors of change in attitudes, needs, psyche etc., will probably never be one hundred percent effective. The coordination of factors in planning so as to maximize freedom of choice represents an approach to problems rather than a final solution. The usefulness of the pattern of a Roman Republic in promoting greater human dignity and the common good thus depends ultimately on the attitudes of the leaders and whether they are willing to balance freedoms in their society.

9

FREEDOM IN A SOCIALIST SOCIETY

To Give According to Need

Poverty, war and insecurity common to our age, have in many ways stimulated the growth of communism, i.e. socialism. When there is widespread need, the planned coordination of efforts is sometimes the only way of dealing with problems. Rationing of foodstuffs, planned domiciles, coordinated work conditions, and centrally directed programs of entertainment are the results. The assumption is that such coordination will eliminate haphazard, *laissez-faire* drift which benefits some while it denies basic necessities to others. In countries like China widespread poverty preceded the takeover by the communists.

Communism has served two functions mainly wherever it has succeeded: one, it imposes a pattern of control designed to solve immediate problems of law and order; two, an accelerated process of industrialization in the countries which they control has been introduced. In some instances like the case of Russia, communism or socialism has succeeded in raising living standards and establishing law and order.

Socialist governments have, however, been criticized for excessive use of force and suppression of individual rights. The measures taken by the Soviet government in the thirties and against various national minorities after World War II indicate the severity of communist government and control.

The communist theory that the state may wither away

after socialism has triumphed and that it then should become possible to give according to need, is controversial, but not crucial for an appraisal of communist practice from the standpoint of the philosophy of freedom. There is a widespread dichotomy between communist theory and practice.[44] Thus, while communist government claims to be democratic, since it derives power theoretically from the people organized in Soviets and cells, extreme delegation of power favors dictatorship and the "personality cult." The Soviet leadership has recently tried to modify the excessive concentration of power by separating functions in the communist party and the Soviet state. To what extent the present move for reform will be successful is yet to be seen.

Economic and social planning in socialist societies has been successful in some respects. Communist practice or socialist practice have led to certain beneficial "by-products" of which the late Pope John XXIII speaks in his encyclical *Pacem in Terris*. Industrialization has, in many cases, solved problems of want, and as a result, poverty and insecurity are not as pronounced as they once were in some socialist states. The price for these reforms has been high in terms of human lives and liberty. Nevertheless, the beneficial by-products of socialist planning must be acknowledged. They may not have much to do with the theory; but in so far as they are facts of life, they must be accepted.

From the standpoint of the philosophy of freedom, economic planning of a socialist variety or any other form is permissible as long as basic human rights are not violated. In Scandinavian countries, Norway, Sweden and Denmark, which are moderately socialist, civil liberties and individual rights have been respected. The same is true for Britain under the Labour government. Moreover, the demand in Russia for greater "socialist legality" since the demise of Stalin indicates that the Soviet people desire greater liberty. The

---

[44] See Father Gustav Vetter in his work *Dialectical Materialism*.

actions of Khrushchev in easing state regulations and abolishing some of the more authoritarian features of Soviet government show that these demands have not been fruitless.

The crucial question is whether any restriction on liberty in a socialist state or society is really necessary. It might be concluded that the criterion "to give according to need" must be applied, in order to measure the need for restrictions on individual liberty. This includes all areas of interest and activity; restrictions on freedom of speech, press, and for that matter, the limitation of the right of property, must be justified in terms of need. If poverty makes some restrictions on the right to property necessary for the welfare of people, then limitation of property rights through taxation, for example, may have priority over individual liberty. The reason is, of course, greater liberty for all rather than any imaginary ideal. To give according to need then means to regulate, plan, restrict, according to need. The criterion of necessity should make arbitrary planning impermissible.

It is a moot question what individuals subjectively need, in order to fulfill themselves. Personal needs vary widely; the standard of need is dependent on checks other than mere subjective judgment. There is no guarantee that many minds will be better than one, or that democratic processes for self-expression will inevitably insure the best results. But "the free market place of ideas" is more likely to reflect what people think is necessary than an abstract formulation of need which can be exploited by a few powerful persons for their own ends. Need is determined from case to case through the free exchange of ideas and the airing of grievances. In that sense, processes for the expression of preferences are essential for freedom in a socialist society.

Freedom and Socialism as a Means

Socialism has triumphed in many countries because of acute problems of need. In China, before the victory of the communists in 1949, economic and social conditions had deteriorated to such an extent that millions of persons were starving or living at a below subsistence level. In other countries, Sweden and England, for example, conditions were not so detrimental as to necessitate violent or drastic change. But the cry for social justice as well as the needs of large segments of the population brought in the socialists and their reforms. While countries like the United States, the Federal Republic of Germany and France are usually regarded as free enterprise economies, they also partake of social security programs and other public services common to socialist states. The kind of reforms or the ways in which freedom is best served is a matter of choice. Depending on circumstances, socialism and capitalism can be regarded as different means toward the same end—greater freedom.

A problem that often arises is how to achieve change which a group or class of persons is able to prevent by threat or use of force. In some of the less industrialized areas of the world today, the resistance of powerful groups to necessary social reforms is one of the main causes for strife. The interdependence of states makes such resistance extremely dangerous, because large power blocs may become involved in local disputes and this in turn may cause escalation toward world war. The breakdown of law and order in any part of the world may create a vacuum into which other powers may be tempted to step, thus creating a danger to peace. The Congo crisis is an example of such involvement.

Nations which have an interest in maintaining the *status quo* may regard socialistic or communistic changes as aggression. Actually, the violence may have started much earlier, namely with the suppression of movements for social change. Nevertheless, as discussed earlier, the Charter of the United Nations and international law forbid recourse to force as a means for social change. Nations are not permitted to intervene in each other's affairs, except in enforcement actions.

A complicating factor is the assistance rendered by one state to another in response to an official invitation. A dictatorship may ask for foreign aid, in order to suppress local freedom fighters. The right to revolution, however, is not restricted to any particular country, but is universal. Standards of non-intervention are significant in as much as they protect peoples and nations against unjustified infringements on their liberty.

In practice, situations involving revolution or as communists would say, "movements for national liberation," can be highly complex. Foreign assistance to local freedom fighters may be interventionist in character. The aim of a foreign power in rendering assistance may actually be imperialistic. Certain activities of major states have been highly questionable in this regard.

In deciding priorities governments may determine that resistance to foreign aggression takes precedence over internal change, if foreign intervention threatens to intensify internal problems. Opposition to internal change which is necessary for the protection and enhancement of human rights and human dignity, would not be justified, however. The timing and manner in which reforms may be executed are questions of operational skill rather than fundamental principle. The important consideration must be greater freedom on the short run or long run, depending on circumstances.

Policymakers may, therefore, be faced with crucial choices involving freedom, when they consider problems of foreign intervention in relation to social change. The only consistent policy would be one which combines protection against foreign intervention with necessary changes for greater freedom.

It has been stated that socialism may be a means for solving pressing economic problems, but—as with all forms of government—can not be an end unto itself. If widespread want makes a certain degree of central control and planning necessary, then socialist means may actually be conducive to greater freedom of choice on the long run. Due process of law or what sometimes is referred to in socialist countries as "socialist legality" has to be safeguarded. As long as socialism is a means in this sense, a means accepted by the majority of the people, it is compatible with the philosophy of freedom.

Socialism can not be imposed on a people. In some cases where social change is resisted by the establishment, socialist governments may come to power through drastic means. In such instances violence breeds violence, and it is almost useless to speculate on who started the process, because its roots usually run deep. Adaptation to the needs of our time is in fact another way of saying protection of rights. The violent prevention of necessary changes is resistance to freedom itself.

Nevertheless, this would not justify suppression of freedom by those who were formerly suppressed; in other words, when socialists have seized power after being suppressed by an authoritarian dictatorship, they may not impose a dictatorship of their own. What they demanded for themselves, namely a voice in the affairs of state, they must be willing to grant to others. Any alternative would amount to a denial of freedom.

It is clear that the policies of socialists differ from country to country. Swedish and British socialists have been willing to abide by democratic processes and to grant the opposition freedom of dissent. In Communist China and the Soviet Union on the other hand, socialism has sometimes been conducive to rabid authoritarianism and the most severe denials of rights. This distinction is of the greatest significance, when it comes to a fair appraisal of socialist practices from the standpoint of the philosophy of freedom. A balanced view of freedom requires recognition of the freedom to oppose a government as well as more effective measures to insure freedom from want.

The excuse that the imposition of socialist reforms by force may hasten "the withering away of the state" and greater freedom on the long run does not hold; socialist dictatorship and Stalinist authoritarianism have not given way to the classless society. In fact, the reforms of Nikita Khrushchev and anti-Stalinism were responsible for greater socialist legality. It is true that in crisis situations restrictions on liberties may be justified, but they must be proportionate and *ad hoc*. The forced imposition of socialist reforms on a people would, therefore, not make socialism a means for greater freedom, but rather an instrument for its destruction. The suppression of the Hungarian Freedom Fighters is an example of this truth.

The Future Society

Karl Marx theorized that in his future classless society man would be able to enjoy the fruits of leisure. Whether or not the ideal of a classless society is feasible, the fact is that leisure is becoming more and more possible for millions of people. Work hours are being shortened, and with growing automation it may be possible, given an orderly transition of the economy, to enable millions more to partake of leisure. The socialist vision of a future society is one of the brotherhood of man freed from the chains of class prejudice and strife, integrated into a human family through ideal cooperative relationships which will succeed the rivaling institutions of previous stages of development. It is in many ways a grand vision, and many persons, young idealists, revolutionaries, etc., have sacrificed their lives for its attainment.

Opponents of socialism maintain that this vision is not justified, because as long as man's nature is what it is, human beings will be subject to rivalries which necessitate government supervision and control. The Marxist ideal of a governmentless society is in practice, however, the justification for strong government leadership during the so-called socialist transition period toward communism. In the Soviet Union as well as Communist China socialist progress has involved authoritarianism. Without dictatorship it might have been impossible for the Russian and Chinese Communists to maintain control of the government. Today these countries are still subject to dictatorial-type governments, and the end of the classless society is not in view.

It has been pointed out that there is a difference between moderate socialists in Sweden and Great Britain, for example, and the Russian and Chinese Communists. British Labourites and Swedish socialists do not emphasize the future vision as much as Russian and Chinese Communists do. They are more concerned with immediate reforms and solutions to problems of need. Furthermore, the British Labour Government as well as the Scandinavian Socialist Governments can not be described as dictatorial, operating as they do under the form of parliamentary democracy. Harold Laski who once opined that the British mercantile interests might rebel against socialist labor reforms, was proven wrong when the British establishment went along with the first British Labour Government under Clement Attlee. The reforms were, of course, moderate by comparison to the changes under Russian and Chinese communism. It might be concluded from this that moderate socialism does not breed as drastic a dichotomy between ends and means as Chinese or Russian communism. This may in large part be due to the different circumstances prevailing in these countries. More drastic needs may be responsible for more drastic reactions.

Leaving aside discussions of future utopias, it is clear that the future society, be it of a socialist, capitalist, mixed, or any other variety, must allow for both individual self-expression and social cooperation. Man the individual is likely to continue to exist, barring unforseen mutations, and the need for social or group cooperation will become more pronounced with the continued increase of world population. The experience of the Russian Communists teaches that socialism should be subject to the restraints of socialist legality; and the press toward greater social justice in non-communist countries indicates that social reforms, i.e. greater freedom from want, fear etc., are necessary in most areas of the world today. Man the individual and man the social being must be granted the greatest possible opportunity for fulfillment in the future society. This involves limitations on arbitrary restraints of human individuality, and the abolition of obstacles and barriers to necessary progress.

This does not mean that there need be absolute agreement on the kinds of reforms required or the kinds of restrictions that must be abolished. The free interchange of ideas in free discussion is the best way of achieving a consensus on necessary reforms and the protection of human rights. In the final analysis, democratic processes are the only guarantee for the survival of freedom everywhere. Freedom of choice must be realized in a socialist society as in any other society. This freedom includes, of course, the right to express political preferences.

10

CONCLUSION—PEACE WITH FREEDOM

AND JUSTICE

In this work it has been shown that the function of government in a free society is to assist the individual members of the body politic in their quest for happiness according to standards which they choose. The need for restraint of freedom in certain cases has been clarified. The objectives of a free society, that is greater individual self-fulfillment, greater human dignity through human rights, have been explained, and ways and means for their attainment described. The importance of cultural and spiritual self-fulfillment have been stressed, and the relation of the different freedoms, that is freedom from want, freedom from fear, freedom of speech, press, worship, etc. to each other examined. In the second part of the work, practical problems for greater freedom have been analyzed in the context of different orders. Freedom in the modern democratic state has been compared to freedom in a socialist society, and the possibility of a Roman Republic in our time explored. The significance of planning in solving basic problems of freedom has been stressed.

The creation of a legal order based on principles of justice has been related to the quest for freedom. The liberation of the spirit of man from unjustified burdens and restrictions has been commended as a necessary task for the attainment of justice. The common good and general welfare were described in terms of individual happiness, and the relation between local and larger units of government clarified. The realization of the philosophy of freedom in the different states and social orders provides the key for a future world order. Interdependence of peoples and nations make cooperation between different social and economic systems mandatory. The dangers of war and nuclear destruction require a greater degree of tolerance and mutual respect between nations and peoples than ever before. Only by promoting greater understanding and recognition of human rights everywhere can the catastrophe of a nuclear war be avoided.

Freedom depends on mutual assistance and cooperation; solutions to outstanding social and economic problems must be sought in terms of mutual rights. Since peoples not nations are the subjects of the future world order, cooperation between individuals is the basis for mutual understanding. The greatest threat to freedom comes from imperialistic, authoritarian elements in society. Peoples of goodwill everywhere need, therefore, to reach out to each other across all real and artificial barriers in order to counteract the designs and ambitions of authoritarian forces. The statement "my country right or wrong" is not permissible; if a country offends against the basic principles of the philosophy of freedom, the tenets of the Universal Declaration of Human Rights, and the general principles of law and justice as recognized by civilized nations, it can be condemned as an aggressor. The hope of the future rests with individuals of goodwill who will make this doctrine of mutual respect and co-existence a living reality.

In each state the final authority must be vested with the people. Individuals who make up the body politic must have the freedom to choose their governments. Economic and social systems may vary, but the people must have the final authority in judging which economic or social system shall govern them. Adaptation to the needs of the times, changes for improvement and progress, must be subject to the will of the people. The most basic limitation on the right of a majority to govern is the right of the minority to dissent. In this sense, human rights of all concerned must be respected. While this ideal may not be attainable under all circumstances, it provides a guideline for policymakers.

The mechanisms for insuring popular control in a state and in the international community may be subject to change. Whether a people governs directly or indirectly is not essential for the realization of the philosophy of freedom. The important consideration is that the executive, the legislature and the courts are in the final analysis responsible to the people. The trend toward greater central control in modern times may be counteracted by greater accountability to the people. The dangers of legislative obstructionism may be countered by mobilization of the populace through referenda or by other means so as to provide a check on the legislators. Arbitrariness on the part of the judges may be prevented by impeachment.

The ways of bringing government closer to the people may differ in socialist countries from those in the Western democracies. But whether the degree of control owed to the people is realized through factory workers' councils as in Yugoslavia, or through self-governing corporations, or through referenda as in France, or through constitutional amendments as in the United States, is not crucial *per se* as long as maximum freedom of the individual is guaranteed and sought by all possible means.

Authoritarianism and imperialism, the projection of authoritarian dominion into foreign affairs, are the greatest threats to international peace in our time. Never before have dictatorships been able to muster such destructive forces. If the world is to live with freedom and justice for all, peace must be preserved under all circumstances. But peace does not depend only on persons of goodwill; it is sometimes necessary to oppose the dangerous, divisive intrigues of authoritarian planners with force. It can only be hoped that the threat of countervailing force, deterrence, and in the end the spectre of the total annihilation of mankind will prevent the forces of aggression from starting a conflict which they will not be able to control. Pope John XXIII in his encyclical *Pacem in Terris* calls to men of goodwill everywhere to unite in the task of building a better, peaceful world. The success of this appeal depends on the concerted, dedicated efforts of men of goodwill to remove obstacles against greater freedom wherever they may exist.

The framework of every discussion involving politics must be the framework provided by the philosophy of freedom. What will be most conducive to greater individual self-fulfillment, greater free choice, greater human rights and greater human dignity must be the questions which policymakers ask themselves before every decision. Tactics may be subject to debate; but these objectives can never admit of compromise. Freedom is indivisible and unalterable. Even when men are deprived of freedom, their basic right to achieve it can never be abrogated; it is part of human nature.

Thus the call goes out to all men to help each other attain greater freedom. Let men rid themselves of the restrictions of poverty. Let them throw off antiquated notions which deprive them of freedom of thought. Let them remove governments and potentates who deny them their basic human rights. Let them look to each other first and to doctrines afterwards. In the final analysis, the philosophy of freedom is nothing more or less than a reaching out of one individual to others. In this spirit let the world prosper in peace with freedom and justice.

Epilogue

EPILOGUE

The practical significance of a philosophy lies in its approach to the solution of actual problems. Instead of starting out with preconceived notions about the nature of community and the public welfare, the philosophy of freedom suggests that individual human beings in relation to each other must be the most important consideration of government and planning in a free society. Man can not live without his fellow human beings; but the welfare of the community must be judged in terms of the happiness of individuals. This means that the extreme of rabid individualism without reference to others' rights must be avoided, on the one hand, and the extreme of collectivist planning without reference to individuals' needs, on the other. The golden mean lies in devising governmental mechanisms and promoting social arrangements which do justice by individuals and their *differing* needs. Man thus achieves freedom within the body politic; the common good is represented by the sum total of individual goods enhanced by what the community has to offer each individual person.

It has been shown that an approach to problems which emphasizes collectivism rather than individual human rights, may lead to extremes of authoritarianism. Thus, if general considerations of welfare are imposed on individuals without regard to civil liberties and human rights, government policy becomes an instrument of oppression. Denials of due process or the equal protection of the laws represent violations of freedom and a betrayal of legitimate authority. Laws and practices promulgated and carried out in pursuit of authoritarian aims would not be valid, because they would be unjust.

Law and order must be directed toward the enhancement

of human dignity, the fulfillment of the individual person in and through the community, and the achievement of the common good through an increase in the overall freedom of every human being, including such needs as freedom from want and from fear, freedom of worship, and what has generally been called the free development of the individual personality. These freedoms are in a sense unlimited in kind since they are basically a reflection of a fundamental conception of human dignity. As man grows and develops in his environment his needs and accordingly, his rights vary.

Thus, wherever there is need for the alleviation of suffering through social planning, goods and services, the philosophy of freedom would sanction appropriate measures to deal with the problems involved. Medical care for the needy, housing for the poor, protection of the citizenry against lawlessness and the advancement of civil liberties, all would represent legitimate concerns under the philosophy of freedom. The *raison d'être* for planning against poverty, oppression, denial of rights, etc., would be greater individual free choice so that diversity may be assured within the community. Deviations from the normal pattern in society would be dealt with case by case. Differences between individuals would be honored as long as they do not represent transgressions of others' rights. Whatever mechanisms are instituted to deal with problems, the main objective must be the enhancement of individual freedom of choice.

Unlike authoritarian philosophies, the philosophy of freedom does not sanction planning for some imaginary goal like the perfect, pure race or the classless society. The reference point of the philosophy of freedom is not a utopia, but the very real needs of persons here and now. Adjustments of claims are made on the basis of fair and impartial adjudication of differing needs rather than a superimposed conception of harmony at the expense of diversity, and this does not mean that long-range planning for the benefit of the community would be excluded. Looking ahead for a moment, there is a school of thought today that anticipates a greater centralization of authority as science and technology make greater inroads in the individual person's sphere of action and thought. The planners of this school do not calculate on greater freedom being the end result of the breakdown of barriers between peoples, but rather an increasing conformity in behavior patterns and actions. Thus, the development of an elite class concept becomes all important in order to maintain what may be considered civilized standards. The common good becomes an abstract entity and lines of communication between persons, community and government are gradually subsumed as matters of state and society grow more complex. Such a negative view of human nature leaves little room for man, the creative human being, to live an existence based on personal choice. The philosophy outlined here is an answer to this trend of thought as well as to the authoritarian philosophies openly competing for attention in the world today. Only by the development of a greater consciousness of human worth and dignity among all peoples will man be able to fulfill himself in society.

The cardinal point of distinction between authoritarian philosophies of whatever nature and the approach represented by the philosophy of freedom is that according to the latter, it is impermissible to impose government and exercise power in violation of human rights. Even though rights may be restricted under certain emergency circumstances, such as war, this can not be done without due regard for the limitations of power. Violations of rights in contravention of generally recognized principles of justice must be considered arbitrary and unjustified, regardless of the purposes which they are supposed to serve. The sacrifice in efficiency which may be involved in a free system must be accepted as the price we have to pay for the preservation of our liberties.

In the United States and Western Europe planning with

due regard for recognized principles of human rights may be more possible than in certain areas of Asia, Africa, and Latin America, where widespread poverty and aggravated needs call for integrated planning schemes in order to effect a transition from tribal to national society. The implementation of these schemes may require the use of force. The pattern of dictatorships in these areas confirms that certain leaders find it more suitable to use dictatorial means of control than to respect civil liberties and human rights under the rationalization that such authoritarian practices are necessary for the achievement of social goals. Such curtailment of rights, however, would only be justified, if the restrictions involved do not represent violations of generally recognized principles of law and justice. The arbitrary imprisonment of persons, denial of fair trial and the imposition of draconic punishments, must all be considered violations of such rights and, therefore, unjustified. The argument that such extreme measures are necessary for the promotion of the common good is fallacious. Nowhere more than in this context does the old adage hold true that "those who live by the sword shall die by the sword." It is necessary for countries plagued by extreme want to devise means for the solution of their problems which do not violate principles of human rights. It is also necessary for countries to cooperate with each other in the alleviation of such want. Only in this way can men achieve a better life with freedom and justice without compromising their integrity and endangering each other's livelihood.

The contents of rights may be always changing, according to different conceptions of social needs; but the conception of rights which can not be abridged by legitimate authority remains inalienable. Thus the task of social planners becomes one of clarifying rights and serving human needs, which involves a healthy respect for *persons* in a happy world. The proper use of power and the prevention of abuses is a condition *sine qua non* for the attainment of this end.

The individual's needs in society are varied; they may be economic, political, psychological, social or personal in nature. A major obligation of the community lies in assisting the individual to free himself from unjustified restrictions. Plans and programs must be devised, therefore, both on the governmental and non-governmental level, to deal with human needs.

In the United States, responsibility builds up from the local to the state and national levels, and problems must be solved on each level. To keep government close to home requires that they be handled on the level most directly connected with the individuals involved. Regardless of whether problems are dealt with on the local, state or federal level, however, the happiness of individuals in the community must be the main concern of planners.

The United States today still suffers from serious food, housing, clothing, medical, and education problems. Government services must be designed, therefore, to free individuals from unjustified restraints on their liberty in these areas or, in other words, to achieve freedom from want. President Johnson's anti-poverty program can be regarded as a milestone in this quest. At the same time, it is important not to lose sight of the need for incentives, both cultural and material in nature, which may stimulate individual creativity and thus promote greater self-fulfillment of the person. The philosophy of freedom requires that freedom of opportunity be given to all and that hunger, destitution, malnutrition, and other inhuman obstacles to human freedom be removed. It also requires that this be done in a manner so as to allow maximum diversity and freedom of choice. Incentives in the form of community approval which may be either material or spiritual in nature, would be necessary to counteract the trend to conformity which stultifies man's mind and body. Persons must be allowed to pursue their own individualistic vision, and children must be encouraged in schools to develop their personal, individual style.

In the area of law enforcement, the community has an obligation to provide protection which will guarantee the safety of citizens from unjustified attacks. Such law enforcement must not interfere with the substantive and procedural liberties of individuals, however. Laws and law enforcement must be designed to facilitate maximum freedom of choice of the individual, and all citizens, whether they be accused or accuser, should receive the benefit of the equal protection of the laws. Law must not be regarded as an instrument for the attainment of some ultimate good; moralistic laws and law enforcement which violate generally recognized human rights are not justified. While persons may make moral judgments, they can not impose them by force. Society must provide incentives for law enforcement officers to respect civil liberties and human rights, and officers who violate such rights should be penalized.

One of the most important areas for the United States in modern times is foreign policy. A burden has been thrust on this country since World War II which has necessitated large-scale global action and world-wide planning through the Marshall Plan, Point IV programs, and the Alliance for Progress. In this field as well as on the domestic scene, governmental and non-governmental mechanisms must operate to alleviate unjustified want and facilitate greater self-determination of peoples. The interdependence of peoples in our time requires dynamic foreign aid programs which must not, however, interfere with the right of self-determination.

In this way requirements of justice are balanced with charity, and freedom from want does not involve imperialistic dominion or suppression of rights. In some cases bilateral aid arrangements may be most satisfactory; but where suspicion of aggrandizement is extremely strong, the services of international organizations like the United Nations may be more effective. Military alliances must not entail domination of a country's internal affairs. Freedom of the individual, freedom of nations, and freedom of peoples who make up nations require a respect for the right of every member of the world community to achieve happiness according to standards which he chooses. The mobilization of the world's resources and services in this cause will provide the means for a more happily integrated world community. The aim is maximum mobility of each individual, greater opportunity for artistic, cultural, creative self-fulfillment of persons, in and through the society of human beings everywhere. This is the essence of the modern human rights movement, the civil rights movement in the South, the Universal Declaration of Human Rights, and the Rome Convention on Human Rights.

The alienation of politics which is the alienation of government from the people, whether they be public governments or private monopolies, local, state or federal, must be overcome through a concerted program for the protection and increase of human liberty in all spheres. Freedom requires a program of action which will weld the people of this country and of the world together in the aspiration for greater opportunity for individual self-fulfillment in creative enterprises that bring happiness and personal satisfaction. To this end, the following five point program is proposed as a practical implementation of the philosophy of freedom in the United States:

(1) Further anti-poverty measures like President Johnson's anti-poverty program combined with incentives through tax deductions or direct rewards for personal initiative in all fields from business to the arts and education. A National Arts Council should reward distinguished productions with prizes; the government might allow further tax exemptions for educational purposes; more housing might be combined with incentives for creative housing designs; medical care might be supplemented with incentives for persons to invest in programs suitable to their own tastes, which may grant greater privacy; excellence in production should be praised and outstanding producers singled out for

honors, etc.

(2) Laws and law enforcement should be reformed so as to allow maximum freedom of the individual as long as he does not violate others' recognized rights. Court room procedures should be streamlined. Moralistic laws like those on prohibition need to be repealed. Prisoners should be treated as citizens and not outcasts, and assisted in a process of correction which should terminate as soon as they are adjudged fit again for society. The community should assist such individuals in the rehabilitative process as well. Thus they should be freed as soon as they appreciate properly the benefits of freedom.

(3) Foreign alliances, aid programs, etc. should be partnerships rather than coalitions of force. Leaders of nations should meet as allies dedicated to the proposition that freedom from want and freedom from fear are indivisible and must be worldwide. They should cooperate with each other in this spirit to thwart imperialistic, aggressive designs, whether they be perpetrated on the national or international level. Goodwill reaches across frontiers, and men of goodwill should assist each other to achieve peace on earth with freedom and justice.

(4) A fourth force should be organized aside from government, political parties, and pressure groups, that is a citizens' movement of America. Citizens' groups should be formed in every locality with the aim of interacting with government and pressure groups, demanding explanations and being educated in turn by the leadership. Thus a more enlightened, active citizenry may be assured.

(5) A Constitutional Amendment should be passed providing for the possibility of a legislative referendum. Thus a sufficient number of voters could challenge the government and promote measures which are nation-wide, and governments in turn could receive popular approval for proposed reforms.

These, in brief, are some of the practical applications of the philosophy of freedom.

Discussion

A DISCUSSION

At The Center for the Study of Democratic Institutions*

ROBERT M. HUTCHINS: The speaker of the day is Mr. Robert Woetzel.

ROBERT K. WOETZEL: First of all, when I speak of philosophy, I am not referring to any particular definition of philosophy. My approach is more political science, government, and public law than philosophy in the narrow sense. Secondly, I'd like to say that this is no blueprint for action. It's supposed to influence attitudes which determine action rather than provide exact guidelines. Thirdly, it is not supposed to be associated with any particular nation; it is not nationally fixed in its emphasis. It is international in its scope; in other words, it has taken into consideration many different historical traditions on both sides of the Iron Curtain. When I refer to such concepts as "socialist legality," I'm also thinking of general concepts of human rights. I have tried to find a common denominator. Fourthly, I don't think we want to get into the question of a definition of "conservative" versus "liberal" these terms have no meaning in the traditional sense. Nor should we get into a discussion on individualism as understood in the nineteenth century. I am speaking of individual in the sense that the word "person" is

---

* Following is the synopsis of a discussion on THE PHILOSOPHY OF FREEDOM which took place at the Center for the Study of Democratic Institutions in Santa Barbara, California, on January 18th and 19th, 1965.

used—in the Universal Declaration of Human Rights or in
the European Convention of Human Rights; in other
words, the individual person. Then, I have used words
like "liberty" and "freedom" interchangeably. I hope the
stricter philosophers here will pardon me for that; I am
not trying to evade an issue, but I think my meaning is
clear.

The basic thesis is that man the individual is the be-all
and end-all of all government; and the aim of man which
I prefer perhaps *a priori,* is the quest for happiness—individual happiness according to standards which he
chooses. In that sense, I stipulate that man obviously can
not be an island unto himself; he needs other human beings—he is a social being. But the social aspect of his nature derives from his individuality as a human being rather than from society; in other words, it proceeds from
the individual and his need for society rather than from
the standpoint of society and the place of the individual
in it.

Furthermore, I understand the common good in terms
of the sum total of individual goods. I do believe that
there is something additional that comes from social interaction; but in the last analysis, the aim of this is the individual good in society.

I contrast justice with law; from the point of view of the
philosophy of freedom, justice reflects more for the attainment of the common good, that is individual good,
than law. Law which does not fulfill the norms of justice
is not only not binding, it isn't even law. It is perhaps
some tribal edict.

Mechanisms of government are instituted to help individuals toward their happiness, *not* the other way around.
Freedom of choice becomes essential for the realization
of individual potential, because of the diversity of human
nature, psyche, etc. Authoritarianism is the anti-thesis in

this context, because it suppresses individual free choice. It is the greatest enemy to the individual. Individuals have the right to throw off government that does not fulfill its proper function. Not only that; they can, in good conscience, disobey laws that are tyrannical. They even have a duty to disobey such laws when they are criminal; that is the lesson that the Nuremberg trials point to. International criminal law as quoted by the United Nations in-, dicates that if law becomes tyrannical there exists a duty, a right, and an obligation to throw it off, and to counteract the individuals who are responsible for it.

What I have tried to do, in effect, is to incorporate the concept of human rights into a philosophy. The movement for human rights is international; individuals reach across fences to each other—Russians to Americans as individuals and *vice versa*—to help each other guard and develop human rights against authoritarian influences in their respective countries. The enemy becomes an authoritarian militarist wherever he may be, in Moscow or the Pentagon. A friend is he who respects the legality of human rights. This is the dynamic process of peace, as I see it.

Planning is essential for the attainment of what has been called "freedom from want," and may, therefore, be regarded as another means toward an end. It never is an end unto itself. Planning is essential in our time particularly, because of the proliferation of problems, social and economic. The limits of authority are judged in terms of necessity; the burden of the proof for any limitation on freedom rests with the restricting authority. Certain extremists will maintain that they do not wish restrictions, for instance, on freedom of speech, press, etc., but on the other hand, they would favor restrictions in the economic sphere for some good; that presupposes on the other hand, that you have so-called conservatives who don't wish any restrictions in the economic sphere, but would impose moral restrictions on personal freedom. In other words, some would legislate for morality, but not in the economic area—and others *vice versa*. I am trying to get rid of this dichotomy by indicating that both points of view are subsumed under the concept of freedom of the individual who needs economic freedom or freedom from want, as well as freedom from fear and suppression of other kinds of rights.

In the area of cultural and spiritual values, the aim is to provide different alternatives for cultural or spiritual self-fulfillment and allow the individual to choose. This is the development of the religious liberty schema in Rome today, if I understood it correctly, and at the same time, the essence possibly of a progressive interpretation of peaceful co-existence, as the Russians mean it. And in that sense, I think here again there is a possibility of a meeting ground.

As far as incentives are concerned, they are not meant in terms of a monetary reward necessarily; but this could play a role obviously. I wouldn't say that the business of America is only business; but I think that monetary or material incentives are just as important as cultural and spiritual incentives for self-fulfillment.

Freedom is then analyzed within the context of different social orders. I go back to the problem of deriving individual choices by one type of mechanism or another, and I define these. I also explore the problem of protection versus achievement, and the two faces of federalism. I reconcile the two in terms of individual freedom and priorities to be settled by the people themselves. The dichotomy between prince and people is overcome in this philosophy, because government has no other needs, no other ends, than to serve individuals. The important factor is that means for citizens' action must be allowed, must be guarded.

In conclusion, I explore the question of the relation of peace to human rights and treat the contention that violations of human rights are steps in the direction toward war and aggression. The Nazi example was a perfect case; in other words, violations of human rights that took place in the thirties eventually led to the cataclysm of 1939.

The basic approach, therefore, is to relate governments, public and private, to man's individual needs, and thus to create a new way of looking at things in our mass society which will enable us to go from the person rather than from some abstract conception of an ideal.

JOHN COGLEY: Do you feel that society, as society, has no end in itself that transcends the sum total of the individual ends of the people then living?

WOETZEL: I believe that there is something separate that society offers; in other words, what comes from social interaction is something more than what individuals are able to achieve. But I do not believe that this is, in itself, divorceable from the individuals who are benefiting from the interaction.

COGLEY: Would you approve of a society being self-conscious about having a purpose for transmitting, for example, a culture that transcends the living, right now?

WOETZEL: My answer would be that such a purpose can not be imposed by force.

W. H. FERRY: What about the Great Society?

WOETZEL: I think as long as basic human rights are not in any way violated, you can legislate as much as you wish for the general welfare; but when the aims of the society are divorced from individuals' happiness, they usually become dangerous. On the other hand, if you want to strive for a Great Society and a great aim and offer it as an alternative, and the people have the right to choose whether they want it for their happiness, whether they believe in it, or whether they need it for one reason or another, then the attempt to sell them on it would be legitimate.

HUTCHINS: And if 51 percent of the people want it?

WOETZEL: If the choice does not involve basic human rights, it would be sufficient; but no percentage of the electorate would justify a violation of rights.

ZELMAN COWAN: When do you have a violation of basic human rights?

WOETZEL: In the international community we speak of violations only when they are very grave. I hope that eventually the world will be more close-knit so that any violation of human rights, even of one individual anywhere, will become the subject of a restraining authority.

RICHARD LICHTMAN: You asked for fundamental criticisms; I would like to make one in a sweeping way: I think the terms used are essentially meaningless, because they are not defined. They turn out to be so abstract, they have no content; it's impossible to come to grips with them. Take the notion of rights; there's no definition here of what an inalienable right is, a fundamental right, human right, or anything else of the sort. There's no discussion of what constitutes a right. Now, very few, if any, rights are absolute, and there's some notion of inalienable rights; what's the relationship between the fact: when it is that rights are absolute and when it is that they are not absolute—when it is that the rights are inalienable? Is there any right that can be specified under no condition to be removed from an individual justly, and if so, what?

WOETZEL: As far as the viability of the approach described here is concerned, it is the standard of day to day action and efforts,—for instance, at the European Commission on Human Rights, the European Court of Human Rights, the International Commission of Jurists, and many other organizations. But it doesn't provide—and I said this in the beginning—a blueprint. However, concerning the approach itself regarding rights and human beings, I quite clearly indicated that the rights of human beings in society are the fundamental basis of what is called the human rights revolution in our time; and that the human being requires respect for human rights for the attainment of his main end—happiness, according to standards which he chooses.

HUTCHINS: Well, the approach would be interesting, I think, if you'd indicate perhaps more precisely what the enemy is, and what the effects are. I could see that authoritarianism is an enemy, and the effect of this would be to minimize and perhaps repel authoritarianism. Take any major issue that is before the people of the United States today, and suppose this philosophy of freedom were adopted. What would the difference be? I had the feeling at the outset that you are against something, and it turns out that you are against authoritarianism. But as we go on to consider all the various points of view around this table, it seems to me that this statement is so general as to absorb them all. I'd like you to suggest something that is *not* okay, or that can't be brought under these rubrics.

WOETZEL: This is a difficult question in terms of cases. There is a spectrum here: from the most extreme cases, for instance, South Africa or civil rights in the South, we can proceed to the areas of, let us say, bureaucratic infringements of individual liberty of one kind or another. And what is not okay is any kind of restriction on individual freedom of choice, which violates what I believe to be the consensus in the international community today. I believe that Article 38 (c) of the Statute of the International Court of Justice, which mentions general principles of law as recognized by civilized nations, is not a dead letter. There *is* a consensus in mankind today. Most priorities, freedom of speech problems, the question of censorship, other issues of this sort, are always being confronted with great difficulty. The Nuremberg Court, for example, had to make decisions on these issues: what was a crime against humanity? With regard to Mr. Lichtman's comments, you couldn't get a broader category than a crime against humanity! And yet, the unanimous vote in the United Nations endorsing the Judgment of the Court, would indicate that they saw something practical here.

No doubt, the individual points where there exists a near consensus would make an excellent study—to compare what the 20th Party Congress endorsed, for instance, as violations of rights of Soviet citizens, with other conferences and decisions of courts. I think you'd come out with more or less what the Universal Declaration of Human Rights mentions, but possibly more specifically defined.

HUTCHINS: Let's take a number of things: let's take federal aid to education and medicare. What light does this philosophy of freedom shed on issues of that kind?

WOETZEL: As far as medicare is concerned, one could approach it from the problem of the needs of the elderly citizens which would justify action requiring taxes, which, in turn, is a restriction on the economic freedom of individuals who have to pay.

HUTCHINS: It could also justify the opposite approach.

WOETZEL: Well, the question here is whether a basic human right is involved; and we agree that taxation, which has been called the most effective means of revolution in our time, is not a violation of human rights, generally speaking.

HUTCHINS: I want to find out whether this philosophy would assist us, if everybody accepted it; suppose half the people here are against federal aid to education and medicare, and the other half take the opposite position. Is anybody's position on any of these issues 'changed by this philosophy?

WOETZEL: First of all, the discussion takes on a different approach: we would not be discussing utopias or ends as such; we would be discussing basic questions of rights. The other day, for instance, I had a discussion with a judge in Los Angeles, who is known to be rather tough on some issues. The discussion could have bogged down right from the start in opposing principles; but by bringing it into the area of the philosophy of freedom, we were thinking in terms of the human dilemma involved and whether the rights, for instance, of people to be safe from attacks on the streets should be balanced in some ways against the rights of negro demonstrations which may create disorder. The balancing process, you see, puts the whole discussion in a different context; we would be discussing then in terms of human rights and civil liberties. This brings me to another point; when Harry Ashmore the other day said that while he favored civil rights very strongly, he was a moderate civil libertarian, I couldn't follow, because the two are for me, one.

LICHTMAN: Well, we don't have a criterion for balance, and that is one of the problems.

FERRY: Bob, you just said that you have added up the balancing process; well, that's what the dialogue is all about— it's a balancing process. I don't see that the importation of this particular approach adds very much to it. I think you might clear this up a little bit for all of us. All the way through your discussion and through your work I have a vision of government as a necessary evil, not as a creative construction of man, and not as something that men take part in themselves, not as something that men can work on and perfect, but as a weight that is just sitting there about to be overbalanced onto the individual in some way.

WOETZEL: My concept of government is that it is a means to an end. No. I wouldn't say that government is evil necessarily, because it can be a very useful means. The end may require greater government which involves some kind of restraining action, for the sake of human happiness, dignity, freedom from want, and freedom from fear. The basic practical issue is that I would like to use government against authoritarian types of limitations which a consensus in the international community recognizes as violations of human rights. I'd like to use it against these kinds of threats, be they economic or social, or moral, for that matter.

FERRY: Who's the enemy here, if it isn't government?

FRANK KELLY: Every individual has, to some extent, an authoritarian drive and a freedom drive, and I think you're projecting out of the individual these two things and saying that one is good and the other is bad.

WOETZEL: If one wants a moral judgment, then that would be it.

COWAN: The trouble with this, as you have formulated it, is that I think I would have read these propositions stated a hundred years ago: John Stuart Mill.

WOETZEL: Well, I indicated at the beginning of the discussion that I hoped I wouldn't be accused of being *too* repetitive. But I think I've tried to pose the perennial problem in modern terms. I do not think that I am saying that much new, perhaps, in terms of the essence of freedom; there were philosophers of freedom throughout the ages.

COWAN: If I could follow up my point, then; we've got to understand this in context. Take fair employment practices; which is the greater right: my right to employ whom I like or . . .

WOETZEL: The question is whether in your approach one policy or another would violate basic conceptions of human rights and in terms of the essence of the philosophy of freedom, provide the liberty of choosing alternatives.

HUTCHINS: Well, the only way you can solve it, as I understand it, is by a vote of the public or on the basis of a discussion along these lines; so that if 51 percent of the people whose rights are at stake here, come to the conclusion that they do not want fair employment practice, then you don't have it.

WOETZEL: I agree with you to a point. But there is one thing more: the concept of individual dignity is imbedded in the very nature of things; regardless of how people vote, it remains valid.

HUTCHINS: Well, suppose people come out on the side of the employee and individual rights?

WOETZEL: A person may reserve the right to disagree.

HUTCHINS: Well, then, if I understand it, you're prepared to assert the right of the individual, the colored man, to a job, as against the right of the employer to determine that he is not entitled to one.

WOETZEL: No; to get back to the question of determining the meaning of rights, I don't think voting is the only way. There are other ways: referenda, citizens' action, even polls help to determine the will of individuals. I shy away from concepts like the "will of the people," because these abstractions, I think, have been the cause of untold damage.

LICHTMAN: I don't feel my question was answered, Mr. Hutchins.

WOETZEL: Rights are fundamental in the sense to the extent that we can determine them. But in terms of the practical working out of the process, it requires constant balancing of interests, needs, and rights. In terms of aims, it becomes, like so much else, a pragmatic effort. I know that this sounds, perhaps, difficult to subsume in some kind of definite category; but I think that the approach here has been basic to international lawyers in modern times, for instance. I find that as soon as the discussion is brought into this framework, a certain effort to try to understand the human dilemma is involved. And this is what I mean by reaching a consensus on the meaning of rights in the practical sense.

STANLEY SHEINBAUM: I wonder, if it wouldn't be helpful to try to approach it, not at the level of practical problems—like fair employment practices and federal aid to education,—but on the basis of differences between systems. As I understood the work, I wondered why it couldn't be used by a variety of systems; we could see where it could not fit South Africa, because there are flagrant violations. This is also true of Nazi Germany. Why could this not be used by, say, Mao's China, or Tito's Yugoslavia, however? And I think it *would* be used by them.

WOETZEL: There's a difference here on issues: the factory councils in Yugoslavia, for instance, supposedly insure a certain amount of democratic control and interaction on the part of the citizens in determining policies and priorities. Now, when a country, or a government, is not willing to sanction such interaction, it is at this point that the right to political expression is violated; here is where Mao Tse-tung could not possibly fit in.

What I'm aiming at also is a method of education and conciliation in the international community which would allow governmental actions to be subjected to critical examination. Someone may claim that "my human rights are violated" anywhere, and the aim would be to determine in fair interaction, if this is so or not. In the last analysis, Mr. Hutchins' point might be correct in a practical sense: the vote of a group could be most indicative of popular choices. The essential truth or justice of the question would remain unaffected by the vote, however.

COWAN: Are you proposing that you could determine the content of a human right by a vote of a group?

WOETZEL: Not absolutely; but for a practical rule of thumb, yes; for example, with regard to the fair employment question that Dr. Hutchins raised, or Proposition 14 in the State of California on the question of selling property: the issue would be to decide if we have done a proper job of dialogue and communication, as Mr. Buchanan is always mentioning here; whether or not basic human rights have been violated; or are being violated by such a Proposition.

COGLEY: How do people decide, the people that are doing the voting, that is? What's the basis of the vote? It seems to me you avoid the issue when you say, well, they vote. Suppose I'm one of the voters, don't I ultimately have to face up to the problem?

WOETZEL: Yes; it may be true that people very often are not informed enough about the implications of an issue that is involved. However, if it is an outstanding issue of one kind or another, for instance, past laws on sterilization in some of the Southern states, there would be a reaction on the part of people.

HARVEY WHEELER: I have the feeling that one of the answers to your problem of explaining to us what it is that is novel and distinctive about your philosophy will be found in a clearer exposition of what you mean by the principle of subsidiarity and the way you conceive of having applied it in novel form from a kind of federal context focused on policies in its origin to, as I take it in your development, an individualization of subsidiarity.

WOETZEL: Well, I think that the statement which you once made that the extension of the subsidiarity principle to the individual is part of the philosophical framework which I'm trying to expound, is fair. However, I think that the mere reference to the subsidiarity principle is not sufficient; in other words, I think it's not sophisticated enough for our modern meaning. One has to stipulate that the lower entity may require an intervention on a higher entity's part, in order to insure the fullest development of the personality of the individual involved. This means that the application of the subsidiarity principle is not *ipso facto* correct; the rights of the individual must always take precedence. They must be balanced against concepts of general welfare and the common good.

WHEELER: You denied in answer to John's (Cogley) question that there was an interest of the commonality as distinct from the interests of the components of the commonality. It seems to me that you place yourself in the dilemma of advocating the tyranny of the majority . . . Furthermore, you can not tell us specifically any content for the human right that seems to override on the one hand, the action of a majority, and at the same time everything is reduced, atomized, and brought down to the individual, and then, again we're round the circle of one man-one vote, each count for one, none to count for more than one.

WOETZEL: Yes; but there is no dichotomy here philosophically between government and the individual members of the body politic. On the question of definitions and what specifically these things mean, I think the problem is that my approach is quite empirical and pragmatic on one level, and absolute on another. In other words, rights are absolute as far as theory is concerned, and relative as far as the practical determination of their content is involved.

SCOTT BUCHANAN: Shouldn't you say then what rights are theoretically absolute?

WOETZEL: You mean to list them?

REXFORD TUGWELL: You'd have to, if you were writing a constitution.

WOETZEL: Exactly. Well, I've tried to refer again and again to certain documents like the Universal Declaration of Human Rights, which I believe come as close as possible to a reflection of this.

BUCHANAN: Yes, but this isn't answering the question. You're still at a practical level, when you do this. If you're going to be theoretical, if you're going to claim this distinction, you've got to answer the theoretical question, it seems to me.

JOHN WILKINSON: Logically: I'm convinced that community and the individual are obverse and reverse on the same coin . . .

WOETZEL: I think that the theoretical standards here can not be defined except in certain general terms; but I agree that you have to indicate them, and I think that I have done that . . . As far as the practical or pragmatic question is concerned, I do not think that one should necessarily juxtapose the two levels, practical and theoretical, in order to draw absolute distinctions. In other words, the Universal Declaration or the European Convention of Human Rights define rights generally, as crimes against humanity, for instance, are defined in international criminal law; these definitions may be vague, but they are subject to interpretation and application by courts and other competent organs.

LICHTMAN: Is there such a thing then as an inalienable right?

WOETZEL: Of course; for instance, the right to life in an absolute moral sense. I think the Declaration of Independence also refers to it in that sense, as a moral right.

BUCHANAN: Is it fair to ask you what life means in that case?

WOETZEL: It wouldn't be very useful to just give you a definition. The question can only be answered in terms of judicial process, for instance.

BUCHANAN: But now you're shifting to a practical level . . .

WOETZEL: Yes; perhaps I'm too much of a pragmatist, but I think it is necessary to relate the practical to the theoretical to get any working model. Otherwise, it's just pie in the sky!

FERRY: I have some genuine questions. You said the means of public control will be different under your philosophy. How different? You indicated that the institutions of the community would not be the same using the philosophy that you are putting forth here. How would they differ? And finally, there is the question of individual rights as seen under the Woetzel glass and the rights of people as counterbalanced against the weapons systems of the civilized world. Because, as I understand it, you must come out as a unilateralist, because you are in favor of the individual first and the transcendence of his rights. Now I'm sure from other discussions that you are not a unilateralist.

WOETZEL: Well, your last point will have to be taken up a little later. I'd just like to say that as far as public control is concerned, I tried to indicate that I'm referring to flexibility of means that will enable government and other organs of authority in the state to ascertain what people want. This is primarily a humanitarian approach.

HALLOCK HOFFMAN: I think I'm asking the same question that other people are asking, but with an emphasis on your idea of what human beings are. As I read your work, it is a discussion of how to achieve the self-realizing society. And at the same time, as several other people have suggested, there doesn't seem to be any society in it. The separation of the individual and isolation of one individual from another seems greater than would be possible if there were to be a society; or, as John (Wilkinson) just said, society and individuals have to be defined in terms of each other and they are really inseparable. And there is one statement, some place or other, that people are composed of two types of drives or impetuses—they are aggressive, which it is best to say in connection with imperialism or authoritarianism; and they are, I take it, the opposite of this, friendly, loving and generous. Is that how you see people as composed of those two elements, at war with each other and having to make some kind of system of controlling their bad qualities and enhancing their good ones? And then aren't those means probably social and how did this get connected to freedom of choice, which sounds to me like an absolutist use of the word?

WOETZEL: As far as the absolutism is concerned, I hope that my commitment, as I said at the beginning, is not interpreted that way. I think that the recognition of differences indicates that that's the heart of the whole thing; I want difference. In terms of what you've asked, I think that from my point of view, man can not be an island unto himself; he needs other people; he needs society. But this need is individual rather than in terms of society. Therefore, man needs the cooperation of other human beings; he needs love, affection. His instincts toward aggressiveness should be combatted; this is what I mean when I say that peace is a dynamic process. I've been led, particularly in view of my studies of aggression and legal concepts of aggression, to start from the standpoint of peace, from the standpoint of the individual, from freedom, rather than from the standpoint of authority and society. Authoritarian aggressiveness is overcome by the human being's recognition of his needs and others' needs in relation to each other. This in turn, ties in with the human rights movement of today, the crying out of people for their rights—sometimes minorities that we don't even know of, people who are suffering because they are not accepted or understood in some way or other. There must be an effort made to overcome the dichotomy between society and the individual, government and the people, that has been created last but not least by well-meaning system philosophers of all varieties.

REV. VIRGIL CORDANO, O.F.M.: I'd just like to make a reflection; it perhaps comes out of the realms of theology rather than all of this. I just wonder if this isn't somewhat parallel to what has happened in the society we call the Christian society of the church. I feel that there is a combination here of principle and the pragmatic element in the Christian society which, I guess, in time became identified with the Roman Catholic Church. There's always a tendency within a given framework, a given society, for the solidification of a given position and this is where the principle is off, because it needed some opposition of what Paul Tillich calls the Protestant principle which serves as a check. And the principle here is needed as a check on a given society which I think tends toward, what perhaps the Roman Catholic Church eventually became before the Protestants came around, and which perhaps may be the end result of the American society. And so, what Tillich has said that we need is Catholic substance—if you want to put it that way—plus Protestant principle. So the right, the only right, really, is self-determination, which would be a variant of a sort of the Protestant principle. I propose that there's some kind of parallel there.

HUTCHINS: I would like to suggest that two questions raised here have received, perhaps, too little consideration: the question whether the individual advanced here is a myth and a myth of an undesirable sort; and the notion that this individual who, it seems to me, is probably mythical, can select for himself whatever he wants to do which seems to compound the myth, and compound it undesirably. This is the basis of the whole structure, apparently; the individual being the person who possesses rights, and his principal right being freedom of choice.

WOETZEL: Before taking up this question, I would like to make a point on Mr. Buchanan's criticism of the theory. I can only revert back to my own philosophical formation in stating that when I speak of inalienable rights, I am actually referring to standards in heaven, more or less; in other words, there is a Greek reflection of these inalienable rights in pragmatic terms, — shadows. And the pragmatic reflection is, then, anchored or expressed in such statements as the Universal Declaration of Human Rights and the European Convention of Human Rights.

Now, as for the question that Mr. Hutchins posed, namely the possible undesirability of the so-called myth of the individual I would answer that by indicating that I think the myth of the individual *not* being a reference point has been extremely dangerous, particularly in modern times. I'm thinking specifically of Rosenberg's "myth of the twentieth century"; or the Marxist myth of a future classless society, — both of which have been responsible for seizures of power and arbitrary exercises of authority. While I do not believe that the individual can exist separately from society — people need each other, — the reference point of any society must still be the individual. Going back for one second to the question of theoretical standards, I think that the argument about these standards, in philosophical terms, can also achieve the opposite of what I am aiming at, namely greater freedom and human dignity for the individual; because when people start to argue in absolute terms about such standards, when they say, "God is on my side" or "God is not on your side," the pragmatic working out of differences becomes extremely difficult. I think this is possibly reflected in the history of our pre-Civil War period. As long as Clay and Calhoun and Webster could discuss business in a pragmatic fashion, I think there was a chance for peace.

I think that the concept of the individual being a myth, just as my concept of the individual being a reality, stems from different views of man's role. Those who regard the individual as a myth see him somehow socially determined, that is by environment and by heredity, usually. The fact that he is different, that every individual is different, is glossed over. Now, the extremist individualistic position, where the individual is alone and the only reference point, is obviously not true. What I am trying to stipulate is that the philosophy of freedom builds on the concept of individual human dignity and human rights in connection with the common good; the common good being conceived as the sum total of individual goods, though it is recognized that the community offers something more than just the sum total of individual interests.

What is the practical significance of my appeal for international cooperation between individuals with the attitudes I have just outlined? To give you an example out of my own experience, many of us have worked toward the agreement restricting nuclear testing in outer space. That has been achieved by men of goodwill, I would say.—And what is *Pacem in Terris* all about, if not an attempt to achieve common ground on the recognition of individual welfare, the primacy of the individual in all proceedings? — The Antarctic agreement is another example: it was opposed by over twenty Senators; the agreement was achieved by men working toward the aim of freeing resources in order to devote them to what was considered greater needs. Priorities, in other words, were determined according to humanitarian conceptions, not by ideological warfare or by authoritarian conceptions of right and wrong. A philosophical discussion would have bogged down immediately in the Congress and would have destroyed the whole basis of an agreement, because Marxism remains Marxism in spite of the pragmatic agreements that we are able to work out. You can't gloss over these difficulties.

Furthermore, I would like to refer to Pope John XXIII's words, when I say complex things can be made simple. If one reads the dialogues of Socrates, they are very simple, at least in the understanding of basic truth. There's no need to go into gyrations or to refer to any particular school.

Finally, when I refer to the struggle of spirit against law, there is no real dichotomy here, when law serves the functions that I have indicated; but the important thing to remember is that the struggle of the individual to find peace and happiness in the community is an unending one. It does not depend on the achievement of an ideal community, as such.

LICHTMAN: I have two comments, one about the problem of theory in practice, and another about the nature of individuals in society.

I think there is a very important and disastrous confusion in theory with regard to these matters. They're not simply matters of definition in any trivial sense. The matter of theory is simply the matter of understanding. One theorizes about rights because one wants to understand what a right is. That's neither absolute, nor pretentious, nor jargonized, nor narrow, nor anything else. If you don't have a theory, of course, all you can do is fall back upon lists of proposals for the naming of given rights, which is what you tend to do. That's not the end of comprehension; that's only the beginning of comprehension. The end of comprehension is to understand first what it is that makes those rights right, why they all appear on a list, whether the group is correct in labelling them all as rights, and what it means by labelling them as rights.

The difficulty that the group avoids, of course, is that it doesn't have to consider the relative significance of those rights in relationship to each other. Now, I propose to you that there are theories of rights where balancing is impossible. If a right is inalienable, it is not a good pragmatic adjustment to balance that right; it's a violation of principle to balance that right. One has to decide carefully from the beginning whether you really wish to maintain the right as inalienable or not. Now, I can give you an instance in theory: Kant was perfectly clear when he stated that it was always wrong to tell a lie. And he added that though it might be useful on occasions, or convenient, or conducive to the general happiness, to tell a lie, one is still obligated not to tell one. To say that we are obligated not to tell the truth on all occasions, but have to lie for practical reasons, is simply to say that we must violate ethical standards, — which is simply an argument for immorality. Now, if you don't want to hold that rights are absolute, then give up the term inalienable and explain in some fashion how it is that these rights are connected with each other. And it doesn't do any good to talk about rights as though they were laid up in heaven and men somehow see only their shadows. That means, simply, that men are not clear about how they should formulate the right, or that the content of the right changes, or that new historical circumstances require a different formulation of the right. But that's all on the side which mitigates against holding that the rights are sharply inalienable, because the content of them keeps altering.

I'll just make the second remark, which is about individuals in society. I'd say you miss two other things: you miss the extent to which an individual is socially impregnated from the beginning. You see individuals as an original category, and then you take these individuals, who are in some sense separate from each other, and you see them coming together: they need each other so they rely on each other and agree to do this or that. But the important and profound consideration is: what is it to be an individual from the beginning? You and I think differently from people in the fifth century B.C. in Athens, or people in the eighth century, or people in China, or various other places; we are individuals, but the nature of what it is to be an individual is obviously impregnated by historical and social factors. I think you lose also, from another point of view, the *end* of what it is to be an individual. I'll make what I hope to be a positive suggestion: I think you fall back on the atomistic view, because you see only one alternative to it, and that alternative frightens you so much that you want to make sure you stay as far away from it as possible. And I think the alternative that you see is that the state is something over and above the individuals. And that view, with its totalitarian implications, that is with the subservience of men to some abstract ideal alarms you so much that you keep falling back upon the ideal of individuals in some additive notion. But there's an alternative, and that is that individuals form a society because they share in common certain relational goods. Now, a relational good is not in addition to goods, but neither is it something which transcends individuals. For example, I would think justice is a relational good. You don't get justice by adding up anything which is individual; you get justice by relating individuals. A relationship is neither transcendent of individuals nor is it simply the sum of them. There are conceptions like "justice" or "beauty" or "love" which can not really be seen as the summation of individual satisfactions, or happiness, or pleasures. If there weren't such an alternative view, then I think you'd be justified in feeling that you're on the horns of a dilemma, and that you either had to choose some abstract totalitarian view which made the state an end in itself, or some kind of atomistic view which simply adds up individuals.

WOETZEL: May I answer that very quickly? And very briefly? First of all, as to what is inalienable, I think it will be impossible to build a bridge between your conception and the position that I take. What I am, in essence, saying is: that the perfect truth, or what you call values such as beauty, justice, etc., is not recognizable in my way of thinking—though, of course, I do not wish to impose that view on any one. There are alternative views, as you have indicated; but the reflection of the attempt to fathom will lead to pragmatic elucidations, statements of one kind or another, like the Universal Declaration, which do not have to get into this problem.

Now, as far as the second point is concerned, Kant said that the individual is always more than a means; he must be an end. Philosophically, that would be the basis of my political theory, in the broadest sense. That does not exclude, again, that there are values such as beauty, which are difficult to comprehend merely in terms of an individual, because, as I've said, the community offers more than just the sum total of individual interests. But still, as an end of community action the philosophy of freedom stipulates the individual's happiness, and not an abstraction in terms of values, like beauty. And this does not in any way conflict with an appreciation of beauty, justice, etc.

Thirdly, there is the problem of the state. I have indicated that a philosophy which provides that the state is to be a means toward the achievement of individual happiness and self-fulfillment is no contradiction, if it becomes synonymous with individuals and their aspirations. There is no abstraction, in other words, that can be separated from individual strivings, according to this framework. In this sense, the dichotomy between the prince and the people is overcome. There is no contract, as such, because everything goes back, theoretically, to the wills of individuals. Government is not an end unto itself, nor is the state, nor the nation. It all goes back to the individual. The only problem is how to realize the wills of individuals, and that, as I see it, is the primary problem of political science in our time.

FERRY: Let us address ourselves very directly to the following question: the state is not concerned only with the welfare of the individual in the state. It is concerned with the welfare of all individuals.

WOETZEL: Yes.

FERRY: Now, it seems to me that the national posture of a state which is preparing genocide — and I'm talking about the United States and Russia — can not fit into this philosophy freedom.

WOETZEL: Since you ask me, I feel that the United States has a great destiny, if it fulfills the precepts of the philosophy of freedom. The statement "my country right or wrong" is no longer applicable either according to the philosophy of freedom or according to international law. If the state does not fulfill its functions according to the international law of peace, it becomes authoritarian and imperialistic; and as such, it must be opposed.

KELLY: Are you saying that because the United States has humanitarian programs, and it comes close to what you think the ideal state would be, it would then be justified to resort to nuclear weapons in defense, because it is the repository of freedom?

WOETZEL: No; all I am saying is that whatever state is fulfilling its legitimate function, and if it is attacked or if individuals as such are attacked anywhere, there is an obligation to help these individuals defend themselves. And I'm not identifying that with the United States alone;

but it could apply just as well to, say, Poland, if it were attacked by Russia or East Germany, for example.

LICHTMAN: You would justify retaliation because of respect for individuals?

WOETZEL: I don't justify retaliation as the achievement and protection of freedoms; but I would justify the use of force, if unavoidable.

LICHTMAN: Can there be a "just" atomic war on the grounds of respect for individuals?

WOETZEL: I indicated here quite clearly that weapons may be used, if unavoidable; but then, I also made the statement, quite categorically, that this is always a lesser good — in a sense — because it involves coercion of free choice.

HUTCHINS: But there is a difference between the kind of weapons that you're talking about and the kind of weapons that Mr. Ferry is talking about.

WOETZEL: Yes, that is true; there are different categories of weapons and the devastation of some is greater than others.

BUCHANAN: Would you talk a bit about the Roman Republic. I'm not sure whether you are taking this as a model, in the sense that people use that word now, and tentative scheme on the way to what you are talking about.

WOETZEL: First of all, I did not mean it as an end, as such; it was one of the alternatives I discussed in connection with democracies of the traditional variety, comparing them also to guided democracies in the less industrialized countries. However, I was very impressed by statements made by de Jouvenal, and as a result, I decided to go into this more deeply.

There is a difficulty here from my point of view, of achieving sufficient popular control in combination with leadership to achieve the common good. And I think the Roman Republic offers a possible alternative here; you would have leadership, hopefully very qualified, and a popular check — possibly through a Senate. However, I also open up the question of other means of popular control, such as plebiscites, referenda, etc. I was much impressed also by de Jouvenal's comment on discussion groups in France that air in deliberation, the problems of the future. And that is more or less in line with the kind of action I've recommended: citizens action. In other words, as I see it, if we have stronger leadership and a veto power, that still does not obviate the function of participation by the citizenry. And, basically, if I'm aiming for anything, I'm aiming for an international citizens' movement or the formation of individual groups that constantly badger the policy-makers and demand explanations, and which, in turn, are educated by policy-makers.

FERRY: Do you want to do away with *bureaucracies?*

WOETZEL: No; new means have to be found for getting the bureaucracy to respond to popular needs and the "shoe fitteth" argument, — to get them to listen and explain. What I would like to achieve, if one wishes to put it that way, is a kind of gigantic deliberation process.

LICHTMAN: Foreign policy is the one place where the shoe can't fit. It is the one place where that argument is the least useful. It is somebody else's foot you are concerned with, not your own.

WOETZEL: If you think that the people might not be qualified in one sense or another, to judge these issues, that may very well be true. But I still think that there is no substitute here. You have to get the leaders to educate the people, to explain. There is no substitute for free choice.

FERRY: The government is people too?

WOETZEL: Yes; the problem is, however, that in our time, government becomes more and more remote, in a Kafkaish sense, difficult to manage and difficult to influence.

I say, let's make them more responsible and accountable to the people.

FERRY: And you say let's limit it and let's participate in it?

WOETZEL: Limitation in terms of need, yes. In other words, government has no function in terms of restriction *beyond* necessity.

HUTCHINS: Well, let me ask you a simple question: it would seem to me that the standard definition of the aim of society is the common good. And the common good is conventionally regarded as a good that accrues to every member of the community, that would not accrue to him, if he didn't belong to it. Now, when you get to talking about the interaction between the individual and the society, you come out at the same point. But you deny that there is this common good, separate in the sense that it *can* be separate from the good of the individual. So, it seems to me that the structure doesn't lead you anywhere, except to accentuate your warning, which seems to me overdone, against authoritarian government. If government is a government for the common good, it will achieve everything you have in view. Therefore, why talk about individual free choice as the basis of the theory?

WOETZEL: If the common good *does* serve the individual welfare, then we are agreed. I think also that there is a certain consensus here on what are basic rights; but the point of departure is to avoid what I consider the pitfall of an abstraction of common good.

HUTCHINS: Well, freedom is just as much an abstraction as the common good . . .

WOETZEL: Well, I think that the individual is the final reference point.

HUTCHINS: But this is also the view of everybody who is for the common good. What's the common good for? It's for the people in the community.

LICHTMAN: In distinction to many other theoreticians, however, Mr. Woetzel continues to define it as the summation of individual goods. Now, that was not Aristotle's view of the common good . . .

HUTCHINS: But using his own language, he arrives at the same point . . . St. Thomas was the greatest exponent of the common good in the medieval period, and he took precisely the same attitude toward law that you take, Mr. Woetzel, reaching it again by totally different views.

WOETZEL: That is correct; but you must see that I do not disagree that in some cases I might end up at the same place as those who advocate the common good at the start. That doesn't bother me; my point of departure is still individual freedom and human rights.

HUTCHINS: But no one would differ on this question of protection of human rights, surely . . . The notion that starting with the common good leads you in wrong directions, whereas individual freedom inevitably would lead you in right directions, doesn't seem to me to be justified.

WOETZEL: Well, in the last analysis, of course, it depends on individual discretion, reason, and the kind of decisions that are made. But I maintain that the practical applications of the different approaches during the past two or three hundred years show that the approach from the standpoint of nation, people, general welfare, etc., is dangerous.

HUTCHINS: Well, I'll concede that . . . However, the period from the Civil War to the New Deal is a period in which the doctrine of individual freedom, as you have advanced it, led to the most serious consequences in the development of the United States.

WOETZEL: I don't think we have ever equalled the Nazi catastrophe, for example.

COGLEY: I wonder why you use the common good as the

justification for the Nazis, and anybody else, in so far as their concept is really quite a different one.

WOETZEL: I didn't mean to imply that the Nazis were quoting the common good in the sense, for example, that Scott (Buchanan) or you use it . . . What I'm trying to say is that the Nazis denied rights of the individual for the sake of some greater good, which *they* thought was the common good.

BUCHANAN: Bob, there's a thing that came into my mind when I was reading you and it does again now; there's a place in the introduction of de Tocqueville in which he describes most eloquently the inevitable development and increase in the notion of "equality" in our Western culture. Are you saying that somehow this theory of yours of individual right is an idea like that one, which is growing, and there is an inexorability about it?

WOETZEL: Yes.

IRVING LAUCKS: Well, all I want to say is that the amoeba emerged from an inorganic world and he was a one celled-animal; strictly individualistic. And he still is; he's survived all this time. I can imagine a discussion group of amoebas talking just about the way all of you have been this morning. But they agreed to form multi-cellular animals; and that began what we call "progress." And we progressed until a thing came along called "man." And that man was another emergent, just like the amoeba. We can't account for all his powers and attributes by the various cells of which he's composed. It seems to me altogether possible that we may be at a point in evolution where something new is going to emerge from this multi-cellular system called man — we call it, perhaps, "soul" or "intellect" or maybe we can even call it this expression "common good" that I've heard around here so much. But, shouldn't we think more in terms of evolution, at least—

about this community of cooperation — than we do about individualists?

WOETZEL: I'd just like to dispel any impressions both of absolutism and extreme individualism; the heart of this framework is the recognition and acknowledgment of differences, diversity; and at the same time, I have tried to stipulate a unity.

With respect to the amoeba, if the eventual result is the reunion of the parts, as the aim of man was stipulated to be in one of the dialogues in Plato's *Symposium*, then I'm certainly in favor of it.

HUTCHINS: Thank you very much.

Appendices

APPENDIX I

Universal Declaration of Human Rights

Preamble

Whereas recognition of the inherent dignity and of the equal and inalienable rights of all members of the human family is the foundation of freedom, justice and peace in the world,

Whereas disregard and contempt for human rights have resulted in barbarous acts which have outraged the conscience of mankind, and the advent of a world in which human beings shall enjoy freedom of speech and belief and freedom from fear and want has been proclaimed as the highest aspiration of the common people,

Whereas it is essential, if man is not to be compelled to have recourse, as a last resort, to rebellion against tyranny and oppression, that human rights should be protected by the rule of law,

Where as it is essential to promote the development of friendly relations between nations,

Whereas the peoples of the United Nations have in the Charter reaffirmed their faith in fundamental human rights, in the dignity and worth of the human person and in the equal rights of men and women and have determined to promote social progress and better standards of life in larger freedom,

Whereas Member States have ledged themselves to achieve, in cooperation with the United Nations, the promotion of universal respect for the observance of human rights and fundamental freedoms,

Whereas a common understanding of these rights and freedoms is of the greatest importance for the full realisation of this pledge,

Now therefore

The General Assembly proclaims

This Universal Declaration of Human Rights as a common standard of achievement for all peoples and all nations, to the end that every individual and every organ of society, keeping this Declaration constantly in mind, shall strive by teaching and education to promote respect for these rights and freedoms and by progressive measures, national and international, to secure their universal and effective recognition and observance, both among the people of Member States themselves and among the peoples of territories under their jurisdiction.

Article 1—All human beings are born free and equal in dignity and rights. They are endowed with reason and conscience and should act towards one another in a spirit of brotherhood.

Article 2—Everyone is entitled to all the rights and freedoms set forth in this Declaration, without disinction of any kind, such as race, colour, sex, language, religion, political or other opinion, national or social origin, property, birth or other status. Furthermore, no distinction shall be made on the basis of the political, jurisdictional or international status of the country or territory to which a person belongs, whether it be independent, trust, non-self-governing or under any other limitation of sovereignty.

Article 3—Everyone has the right to life, liberty and security of person.

Article 4—No one shall be held in slavery or servitude; slavery and the slave trade shall be prohibited in all their forms.

Article 5—No one shall be subjected to torture or to cruel, inhuman or degrading treatment or punishment.

Article 6—Everyone has the right to recognition everywhere as a person before the law.

Article 7—All are equal before the law and are entitled without any discrimination to equal protection of the law. All are entitled to equal protection against any discrimination in violation of this Declaration and against any incitement to such discrimination.

Article 8—Everyone has the right to an effective remedy by the competent national tribunal for acts violating the fundamental rights granted him by the constitution or by law .

Article 9—No one shall be subjected to arbitrary arrest, detention or exile.

Article 10—Everyone is entitled in full equality to a fair and public hearing by an independent and impartial tribunal, in the determination of his rights and obligations and of any criminal charge against him.

Article 11— (1) Everyone charged with a penal offence has the right to be presumed innocent until proved guilty according to law in a public trial at which he has had all the guarantees necessary for his defence.

(2) No one shall be held guilty of any penal offence on account of any act or omission which did not constitute a penal offence, under national or international law, at the time when it was committed. Nor shall a heavier penalty be imposed than the one that was applicable at the time the penal offence was committed.

Article 12—No one shall be subjected to arbitrary interference with his privacy, family, home or correspondence, nor to attacks upon his honour and reputation. Everyone has the right to the protection of the law against such interference or attacks.

Article 13—(1) Everyone has the right to freedom of movement and residence within the borders of each state.

(2) Everyone has the right to leave any country, including his own, and to return to his country.

Article 14—(1) Everyone has the right to seek and to enjoy in other countries asylum from persecution.

(2) This right may not be invoked in the case of. prosecutions genuinely arising from non-political crimes or from acts contrary to the purposes and principles of the United Nations.

Article 15—(1) Everyone has the right to a nationality.

(2) No one shall be arbitrarily deprived of his nationality nor denied the right to change his nationality.

Article 16—(1) Men and women of full age, without any limitations due to race, nationality or religion, have the right to marry and to found a family. They are entitled to equal rights as to marriage, during marriage and at its dissolution.

(2) Marriage shall be entered into only with the free and full consent of the intending spouses.

(3) The family is the natural and fundamental group unit of society and is entitled to protection by society and the State.

Article 17—(1) Everyone has the right to own property alone as well as in association with others.

(2) No one shall be arbitrarily deprived of his property.

Article 18—Everyone has the right to freedom of thought, conscience and religion; this right includes freedom to change his religion or belief, and freedom, either alone or in community with others and in public or private, to manifest his religion or belief in teaching, practice, worship and observance.

Article 19—Everyone has the right to freedom of opinion and expression; this right includes freedom to hold opinions without interference and to seek, receive and impart information and ideas through any media and regardless of frontiers.

Article 20—(1) Everyone has the right to freedom of peaceful assembly and association.

(2) No one may be compelled to belong to an association.

Article 21—(1) Everyone has the right to take part in the government of his country, directly or through freely chosen representatives.

(2) Everyone has the right of equal access to public service in his country.

(3) The will of the people shall be the basis of the authority of government; this will shall be expressed in periodic and genuine elections which shall be by universal and equal suffrage and shall be held by secret vote or by equivalent free voting procedures.

Article 22—Everyone, as a member of society, has the right to social security and is entitled to realization, through national effort and international cooperation and in accordance with the organization and resources of each State, of the economic, social and cultural rights indispensable for his dignity and the free development of his personality.

Article 23—(1) Everyone has the right to work, to free choice of employment, to just and favourable conditions of work and to protection against unemployment.

(2) Everyone, without any discrimination, has the right to equal pay for equal work.

(3) Everyone who works has the right to just and favourable remuneration insuring for himself and his family an existence worthy of human dignity, and supplemented, if necessary, by other means of social protection.

(4) Everyone has the right to form and to join unions for the protection of his interests.

Article 24—Everyone has the right to rest and leisure, including reasonable limitation of working hours and periodic holidays with pay.

Article 25—(1) Everyone has the right to a standard of living adequate for the health and well-being of himself and of his family, including food, clothing, housing and medical care and necessary social services, and the right to security in the event of unemployment, sickness, disability, widowhood, old age or other lack of livelihood in circumstances beyond his control.

(2) Motherhood and childhood are entitled to special care and assistance. All children, whether born in or out of wedlock, shall enjoy the same social protection.

Article 26—(1) Everyone has the right to education. Education shall be free, at least in the elementary and fundamental stages. Elementary education shall be compulsory. Technical and professional education shall be made generally available and higher education shall be equally accessible to all on the basis of merit.

(2) Education shall be directed to the full development of the human personality and to the strengthening of respect for human rights and fundamental freedoms. It shall promote understanding, tolerance and friendship among all nations, racial or religious groups, and shall further the activities of the United Nations for the maintenance of peace.

(3) Parents have a prior right to choose the kind of education that shall be given to their children.

Article 27—(1) Everyone has the right freely to participate in the cultural life of the community, to enjoy the arts and to share in scientific advancement and its benefits.

(2) Education shall be directed to the full development of the material interests resulting from any scientific, literary or artistic producion of which he is the author.

Article 28—Everyone is entitled to a social and international order in which the rights and freedoms set forth in this Declaration can be fully realised.

Article 29—(1) Everyone has duties to the community in which alone the free and full development of his personality is possible.

(2) In the exercise of his rights and freedoms, everyone shall be subject only to such limitations as are determined by law solely for the purpose of securing due recognition and respect for the rights and freedoms of others and of meeting the just requirements of morality, public order and the general welfare in a democratic society.

(3) These rights and freedoms may in no case be exercised contrary to the purposes and principles of the United Nations.

Article 30—Nothing in this Declaration may be interpreted as implying for any State, group or person any right to engage in any activity or to perform any act aimed at the destruction of any of the rights and freedoms set forth herein.

APPENDIX II

European Convention for the Protection of Human Rights and Fundamental Freedoms

The Governments signatory hereto, being Members of the Council of Europe,

Considering the Universal Declaration of Human Rights proclaimed by the General Assembly of the United Nations on 10th December 1948;

Considering that this Declaration aims at securing the universal and effective recognition and observance of the Rights therein declared; ....

Considering that the aim of the Council of Europe is the achievement of greater unity between its Members and that one of the methods by which that aim is to be pursued is the maintenance and further realisation of Human Rights and Fundamental Freedoms;

Reaffirming their profound belief in those Fundamental Freedoms which are the foundation of justice and peace in the world and are best maintained on the one hand by an effective political democracy and on the other by a common understanding and observance of the Human Rights upon which they depend;

Being resolved, as the Governments of European countries which are like-minded and have a common heritage of political traditions, ideals, freedom and the rule of law, to take the first steps for the collective enforcement of certain of the Rights stated in the Universal Declaration;

Have agreed as follows:

Article 1—The High Contracting Parties shall secure to everyone within their jurisdiction the rights and freedoms defined in Section I of this Convention.

SECTION I

Article 2—(1)Everyone's right to life shall be protected by law. No one shall be deprived of his life intentionally save in the execution of a sentence of a court following his conviction of a crime for which this penalty is provided by law.

(2) Deprivation of life shall not be regarded as inflicted in contravention of this Article when it results from the use of force which is no more than absolutely necessary:

(a) in defence of any person from unlawful violence;

(b) in order to effect a lawful arrest or to prevent the escape of a person lawfully detained;

(c) in action lawfully taken for the purpose of quelling a riot or insurrection.

Article 3—No one shall be subjected to torture or to inhuman or degrading treatment or punishment.

Article 4—(1) No one shall be held in slavery or servitude. (2) No one shall be required to perform forced or compulsory labour. (3) For the purpose of this Article the term "forced or compulsory labour" shall not include:

(a) any work required to be done in the ordinary course of detention imposed according to the provisions of Article 5 of this Convention or during conditional release from such detention;

(b) any service of a military character or, in case of conscientious objectors in countries where they are recognized, service exacted instead of compulsory military service;

(c) any service exacted in case of an emergency or calamity threatening the life or well-being of the community;

(d) any work or service which forms part of normal civic obligations.

Article 5—(1) Everyone has the right to liberty and security of person. No one shall be deprived of his liberty save in the following cases and in accordance with a procedure prescribed by law:

(a) the lawful detention of a person after conviction by a competent court;

(b) the lawful arrest or detention of a person for non-compliance with the lawful order of a court or in order to secure the fulfillment of any obligation prescribed by law;

(c) the lawful arrest or detention of a person effected for the purpose of bringing him before the competent legal authority on reasonable suspicion of having committed an offence or when it is reasonably considered necessary to prevent his committing an offence or fleeing after having done so;

(d) the detention of a minor by lawful order for the purpose of educational supervision or his lawful detention for the purpose of bringing him before the competent legal authority;

(e) the lawful detention of persons for the prevention of the spreading of infectious diseases, of persons of unsound mind, alcoholics or drug addicts or vagrants;

(f) the lawful arrest or detention of a person to prevent his effecting an unauthorised entry into the country or of a person against whom action is being taken with a view to deportation or extradition.

(2) Everyone who is arrested shall be informed promptly, in a language which he understands, of the reasons for his arrest and of any charge against him.

(3) Everyone arrested or detained in accordance with the provisions of paragraph 1 (c) of this Article shall be brought promptly before a judge or other officer authorised by law to exercise judicial power and shall be entitled to trial within a reasonable time or to release pending trial. Release may be conditioned by guarantees to appear for trial.

(4) Everyone who is deprived of his liberty by arrest or detention shall be entitled to take proceedings by which the lawfulness of his detention shall be decided speedily by a court and his release ordered if the detention is not lawful.

(5) Everyone who has been the victim of arrest or detention in contravention of the provisions of this Article shall have an enforceable right to compensation.

Article 6— (1) In the determination of his civil rights and obligations or of any criminal charge against him, everyone is entitled to a fair and public hearing within a reasonable time by an independent and impartial tribunal established by law. Judgment shall be pronounced publicly but the press and public may be excluded from all or part of the trial in the interests of morals, public order or national security in a democratic society, where the interests of juveniles or the protection of the private life of the parties so require, or to the extent strictly necessary in the opinion of the court in special circumstances where publicity would prejudice the interests of justice.

(2) Everyone charged with a criminal offence shall be presumed innocent until proved guilty according to law.

(3) Everyone charged with a criminal offence has the following minimum rights:

(a) to be informed promptly, in a language which he understands and in detail, of the nature and cause of the accusation against him;

(b) to have adequate time and facilities for the preparation of his defence;

(c) to defend himself in person or through legal assistance of his own choosing or, if he has not sufficient means to pay for legal assistance, to be given it free when the interests of justice so require;

(d) to examine or have examined witnesses against him and to obtain the attendance and examination of witnesses on his behalf under the same conditions as witnesses against him;

(e) to have the free assistance of an interpreter if he cannot understand or speak the language used in court.

Article 7—(1) No one shall be held guilty of any criminal offence on account of any act or ommission which did not constitute a criminal offence under national or international law at the time when it was committed. Nor shall a heavier penalty be imposed than the one that was applicable at the time the criminal offence was committed.

(2) This Article shall not prejudice the trial and punishment of any person for any act or omission which, at the time when it was committed, was criminal according to the general principles of law recognised by civilised nations.

Article 8—(1) Everyone has the right to respect for his private and family life, his home and his correspondence.

(2) There shall be no interference by a public authority with the exercise of this right except such as is in accordance with the law and is necessary in a democratic society in the interests of national security, public safety or the economic well-being of the country, for the prevention of disorder or crime, for the protection of health or morals, or for the protection of the rights and freedoms of others.

Article 9—(1) Everyone has the right to freedom of thought, conscience and religion; this right includes freedom to change his religion or belief and freedom, either alone or in community with others and in public or private, to manifest his religion or belief, in worship, teaching, practice and observance.

(2) Freedom to manifest one's religion or beliefs shall be subject only to such limitations as are prescribed by law and are necessary in a democratic society in the interests of public safety, for the protection of public order, health or morals, or for the protection of the rights and freedoms of others.

Article 10—Everyone has the right to freedom of expression. This right shall include freedom to hold opinions and to receive and impart information and ideas without interference by public authority and regardless of frontiers. This Article shall not prevent States from requiring the licensing of broadcasting, television or cinema enterprises.

(2) The exercise of these freedoms, since it carries with it duties and responsibilities, may be subject to such formalities, conditions, restrictions or penalties as are prescribed by law and are necessary in a democratic society, in the interests of national security, territorial integrity or public safety, for the prevention of disorder or crime, for the protection of health or morals, for the protection of the reputation or rights of others, for preventing the disclosure of information received in confidence, or for maintaining the authority and impartiality of the judiciary.

Article 11—(1) Everyone has the right to freedom of peaceful assembly and to freedom of association with others, including the right to form and to join trade unions for the protection of his interests.

(2) No restrictions shall be placed on the exercise of these rights other than such as are prescribed by law and are necessary in a democratic society in the interests of national security or public safety, for the prevention of disorder or crime, for the protection of health or morals or for the protection of the rights and freedoms of others. This Article shall not prevent the imposition of lawful restrictions of the exercise of these rights by members of the armed forces, of the police or of the administration of the State.

Article 12—Men and women of marriageable age have the right to marry and to found a family, according to the national laws governing the exercise of this right.

Article 13—Everyone whose rights and freedoms as set forth in this Convention are violated shall have an effective remedy before a national authority notwithstanding that the violation has been committed by persons acting in an official capacity.

Article 14—The enjoyment of the rights and freedoms set forth in this Convention shall be secured without discrimination on any ground such as sex, race, colour, language, religion, political or other opinion, national or social origin, association with a national minority, property, birth or other status.

Article 15—(1) In time of war or other public emergency threatening the life of the nation any High Contracting Party may take measures derogating from its obligations under this Convention to the extent strictly required by the exigencies of the situation, provided that such measures are not inconsistent with its other obligations under international law.

(2) No derogation from Article 2, except in respect of deaths resulting from lawful acts of war, or from Articles 3, 4 (paragraph 1) and 7 shall be made under this provision.

(3) Any High Contracting Party availing itself of this right of derogation shall keep the Secretary-General of the Council of Europe fully informed of the measures which it has taken and the reasons therefor. It shall also inform the Secretary-General of the Council of Europe when such measures have ceased to operate and the provisions of the Convention are again being fully executed.

Article 16—Nothing in Article 10, 11 and 14 shall be regarded as preventing High Contracting Parties from imposing restrictions on the political activity of aliens.

Article 17—Nothing in this Convention may be interpreted as implying for any State, group or person any right to engage in any activity or perform any act aimed at the destruction of any of the rights and freedoms set forth herein or at their limitation to a greater extent than is provided for in the Convention.

Article 18—The restrictions permitted under this Convention to the said rights and freedoms shall not be applied for any purpose other than those for which they have been prescribed.

SECTION II

Article 19—To ensure the observance of the engagements undertaken by the High Contracting Parties in the present Convention, there shall be set up:

(1) A European Commission of Human Rights hereinafter referred to as "the Commission";

(2) A European Court of Human Rights, hereinafter referred to as "the Court".

SECTION III

Article 20—The Commission shall consist of a number of members equal to that of the High Contracting Parties. Not two members of the Commission may be nationals of the same State.

Article 21—(1) The members of the Commission shall be elected by the Committee of Ministers by an absolute majority of votes, from a list of names drawn up by the Bureau of the Consultative Assembly; each group of the Representatives of the High Contracting Parties in the Consultative Assembly shall put forward three candidates, of whom two at least shall be its nationals.

(2) As far as applicable, the same procedure shall be followed to complete the Commission in the event of other States subsequently becoming Parties to this Convention, and in filling casual vacancies.

Article 22—(1) The members of the Commission shall be elected for a period of six years. They may be re-elected. However, of the members elected at the first election, the terms of seven members shall expire at the end of three years.

(2) The members whose terms are to expire at the end of the initial period of three years shall be chosen by lot by the Secretary-General of the Council of Europe immediately after the first election has been completed.

(3) A member of the Commission elected to replace a member whose term of office has not expired shall hold office for the remainder of his predecessor's term.

(4) The members of the Commission shall hold office until replaced. After having been replaced, they shall continue to deal with such cases as they already have under consideration.

Article 23—The members of the Commission shall sit on the Commission in their individual capacity.

Article 24—Any High Contracting Party may refer to the Commission, through the Secretary-General of the Council of Europe, any alleged breach of the provisions of the Convention by another High Contracting Party.

Article 25—(1) The Commission may receive petitions addressed to the Secretary-General of the Council of Europe from any person, non-governmental organisation or group of individuals claiming to be the victim of a violation by one of the High Contracting Parties of the rights set forth in this Convention, provided that the High Contracting Party against which the complaint has been lodged has declared that it recognises the competence of the Commission to receive such petitions. Those of the High Contracting Parties who have made such a declaration undertake not to hinder in any way the effective exercise of this right.

(2) Such declarations may be made for a specific period.

(3) The declarations shall be deposited with the Secretary-General of the Council of Europe who shall transmit copies thereof to the High Contracting Parties and publish them.

(4) The Commission shall only exercise the powers provided for in this Article when at least six High Contracting Parties are bound by declarations made in accordance with the preceding paragraphs.

Article 26—The Commission may only deal with the matter after all domestic remedies have been exhausted, according to the generally recognised rules of international law, and within a period of six months from the date on which the final decision was taken.

Article 27—(1) The Commission shall not deal with any petition submitted under Article 25 which

(a) is anonymous, or

(b) is substantially the same as a matter which has already been examined by the Commission or has already been submitted to another procedure of international investigation or settlement and if it contains no relevant new information.

(2) The Commission shall consider inadmissible any petition submitted under Article 25 which it considers incompatible with the provisions of the present Convention, manifestly illfounded, or an abuse of the right of petition.

(3) The Commission shall reject any petition referred to it which it considers inadmissible under Article 26.

Article 28—In the event of the Commission accepting a petition referred to it:
  (a) it shall, with a view to ascertaining the facts, undertake together with the representatives of the parties an examination of the petition and, if need be, an investigation, for the effective conduct of which the States concerned shall furnish all necessary facilities, after an exchange of views with the Commission;
  (b) it shall place itself at the disposal of the parties concerned with a view to securing a friendly settlement of the matter on the basis of respect for Human Rights as defined in this Convention.

Article 29—(1) The Commission shall perform the functions set out in Article 28 by means of a Sub-Commission consisting of seven members of the Commission.

(2) Each of the parties concerned may appoint as members of this Sub-Commission a person of its choice.

(3) The remaining members shall be chosen by lot in accordance with arrangements prescribed in the Rules of Procedure of the Commission.

Article 30—If the Sub-Commission succeeds in effecting a friendly settlement in accordance with Article 28, it shall draw up a Report which shall be sent to the States concerned, to the Committee of Ministers and to the Secretary-General of the Council of Europe for publication. This Report shall be confined to a brief statement of the facts and of the solution reached.

Article 31—(1) If a solution is not reached, the Commission shall draw up a Report on the facts and state its opinion as to whether the facts found disclose a breach by the State concerned of its obligations under the Convention. The opinions of all the members of the Commission on this point may be stated in the Report.

(2) The Report shall be transmitted to the Committee of Ministers. It shall also be transmitted to the States concerned, who shall not be at liberty to publish it.

(3) In transmitting the Report to the Committee of Ministers the Commission may make such proposals as it thinks fit.

Article 32—(1) If the question is not referred to the Court in accordance with Article 48 of this Convention within a period of three months from the date of the transmission of the Report to the Committee of Ministers, the Committee of Ministers shall decide by a majority of two-thirds of the members entitled to sit on the Committee whether there has been a violation of the Convention.

(2) In the affirmative case the Committee of Ministers shall prescribe a period during which the High Contracting Party concerned must take the measures required by the decision of the Committee of Ministers.

(3) If the High Contracting Party concerned has not taken satisfactory measures within the prescribed period, the Committee of Ministers shall decide by the majority provided for in paragraph (1) above what effect shall be given to its original decision and shall publish the Report.

(4) The High Contracting Parties undertake to regard as binding on them any decision which the Committee of Ministers may take in application of the preceding paragraphs.

Article 33—The Commission shall meet in camera.

Article 34—The Commission shall take its decisions by a majority of the Members present and voting; the Sub-Commission shall take its decisions by a majority of its members.

Article 35—The Commission shall meet as the circumstances require. The meetings shall be convened by the Secretary-General of the Council of Europe.

Article 36—The Commission shall draw up its own rules of procedure.

Article 37—The secretariat of the Commission shall be provided by the Secretary-General of the Council of Europe.

SECTION IV

Article 38—The European Court of Human Rights shall consist of a number of judges equal to that of the Members of the Council of Europe. No two judges may be nationals of the same State.

Article 39—(1) The members of the Court shall be elected by the Consultative Assembly by a majority of the votes cast from a list of persons nominated by the Members of the Council of Europe; each Member shall nominate three candidates, of whom two at least shall be its nationals.

(2) As far as applicable, the same procedure shall be followed to complete the Court in the event of the admission of new Members of the Council of Europe, and in filling casual vacancies.

(3) The candidates shall be of high moral character and must either possess the qualifications required for appointment to high judicial office or be juris-consults of recognised competence.

Article 40—(1) The members of the Court shall be elected for a period of nine years. They may be re-elected. However, of the members elected at the first election the terms of four members shall expire at the end of three years, and the terms of four more members shall expire at the end of six years.

(2) The members whose terms are to expire at the end of the initial periods of three and six years shall be chosen by lot by the Secretary-General immediately after the first election has been completed.

(3) A member of the Court elected to replace a member whose term of office has not expired shall hold office for the remainder of his predecessor's term.

(4) The members of the Court shall hold office until replaced. After having been replaced, they shall continue to deal with such cases as they already have under consideration.

Article 41—The Court shall elect its President and Vice-President for a period of three years. They may be re-elected.

Article 42—The members of the Court shall receive for each day of duty a compensation to be determined by the Committee of Ministers.

Article 43—For the consideration of each case brought before it the Court shall consist of a Chamber composed of seven judges. There shall sit as an *ex officio* member of the Chamber the judge who is a national of any State party concerned, or, if there is none, a person of its choice who shall sit in the capacity of judge; the names of the other judges shall be chosen by lot by the President before the opening of the case.

Article 44—Only the High Contracting Parties and the Commission shall have the right to bring a case before the Court.

Article 45—The jurisdiction of the Court shall extend to all cases concerning the interpretation and application of the present Convention which the High Contracting Parties or the Commission shall refer to it in accordance with Article 48.

Article 46—(1) Any of the High Contracting Parties may at any time declare that it recognises as compulsory *ipso facto* and without special agreement the jurisdiction of the Court in all matters concerning the interpretation and application of the present Convention.

(2) The declarations referred to above may be made unconditionally or on condition of reciprocity on the part of several or certain other High Contracting Parties or for a specified period.

(3) These declarations shall be deposited with the Secretary-General of the Council of Europe who shall transmit copies thereof to the High Contracting Parties.

Article 47—The Court may only deal with a case after the Commission has acknowledged the failure of efforts for a friendly settlement and within the period of three months provided for in Article 32.

Article 48—The following may bring a case before the Court, provided that the High Contracting Party concerned, if there is only one, or the High Contracting Parties concerned, if there is more than one, are subject to the compulsory jurisdiction of the Court or, failing that, with the consent of the High Contracting Party concerned, if there is only one, or of the High Contracting Parties concerned if there is more than one:

  (a) The Commission;
  (b) a High Contracting Party whose national is alleged to be a victim;
  (c) a High Contracting Party which referred the case to the Commission;
  (d) a High Contracting Party against which the complaint has been lodged.

Article 49—In the event of dispute as to whether the Court has jurisdiction, the matter shall be settled by the decision of the Court.

Article 50—If the Court finds that a decision or a measure taken by a legal authority or any other authority of a High Contracting Party is completely or partially in conflict with the obligations arising from the present Convention, and if the internal law of the said Party allows only partial reparation to be made for the consequences of this decision or measure, the decisions of the Court shall, if necessary, afford just satisfaction to the injured party.

Article 51—(1) Reasons shall be given for the judgment of the Court.

(2) If the judgment does not represent in whole or in part the unanimous opinion of the judges, any judge shall be entitled to deliver a separate opinion.

Article 52—The judgment of the Court shall be final.

Article 53—The High Contracting Parties undertake to abide by the decision of the Court in any case to which they are parties.

Article 54—The judgment of the Court shall be transmitted to the Committee of Ministers which shall supervise its execution.

Article 55—The Court shall draw up its own rules and shall determine its own procedure.

Article 56—(1) The first election of the members of the Court shall take place after the declarations by the High Contracting Parties mentioned in Article 46 have reached a total of eight.

(2) No case can be brought before the Court before this election.

SECTION V

Article 57—On receipt of a request from the Secretary-General of the Council of Europe any High Contracting Party shall furnish an explanation of the manner in which its internal law ensures the effective implementation of any of the provisions of this Convention.

Article 58—The expenses of the Commission and the Court shall be borne by the Council of Europe.

Article 59—The members of the Commission and of the Court shall be entitled, during the discharge of their functions, to the privileges and immunities provided for in Article 40 of the Statute of the Council of Europe and in the agreements made thereunder.

Article 60—Nothing in this Convention shall be construed as limiting or derogating from any of the human rights and fundamental freedoms which may be ensured under the laws of any High Contracting Party or under any other agreement to which it is a Party.

Article 61—Nothing in this Convention shall prejudice the powers conferred on the Committee of Ministers by the Statute of the Council of Europe.

Article 62—The High Contracting Parties agree that, except by special agreement, they will not avail themselves of treaties, conventions or declarations in force between them for the purpose of submitting, by way of petition, a dispute arising out of the interpretation or application of this Convention to a means of settlement other than those provided for in this Convention.

Article 63—(1) Any State may at the time of its ratification or at any time thereafter declare by notification addressed to the Secretary-General of the Council of Europe that the present Convention shall extend to all or any of the territories for whose international relations it is responsible.

(2) The Convention shall extend to the territory or territories named in the notification as from the thirtieth day after the receipt of this notification by the Secretary-General of the Council of Europe.

(3) The provisions of this Convention shall be applied in such territories with due regard, however, to local requirements.

(4) Any State which has made a declaration in accordance with paragraph 1 of this Article may at any time thereafter declare on behalf of one or more of the territories to which the declaration relates that it accepts the competence of the Commission to receive petitions from individuals, non-governmental organizations or groups of individuals in accordance with Article 25 of the present Convention.

Article 64—(1) Any State may, when signing this Convention or when depositing its instrument of ratification, make a reservation in respect of any particular provision of the Convention to the extent that any law then in force in its territory is not in conformity with the provision. Reservations of a general character shall not be permitted under this Article.

(2) Any reservation made under this Article shall contain a brief statement of the law concerned.

Article 65—(1) A High Contracting Party may denounce the present Convention only after the expiry of five years from the date on which it became a Party to it and after six months' notice contained in a notification addressed to the Secretary-General of the Council of Europe, who shall inform the other High Contracting Parties.

(2) Such a denunciation shall not have the effect of releasing the High Contracting Party concerned from its obligations under this Convention in respect of any act which, being capable of constituting a violation of such obligations, may have been performed by it before the date at which the denunciation became effective.

(3) Any High Contracting Party which shall cease to be a Member of the Council of Europe shall cease to be a Party to this Convention under the same conditions.

(4) The Convention may be denounced in accordance with the provisions of the preceding paragraphs in respect of any territory to which it has been declared to extend under the terms of Article 63.

Article 66—(1) This Convention shall be open to the signature of the Members of the Council of Europe. It shall be ratified. Ratification shall be deposited with the Secretary-General of the Council of Europe.

(2) The present Convention shall come into force after the deposit of ten instruments of ratification.

(3) As regards any signatory ratifying subsequently, the Convention shall come into force at the date of the deposit of its instrument of ratification.

(4) The Secretary-General of the Council of Europe shall notify all the Members of the Council of Europe of the entry into force of the Convention, the names of the High Contracting Parties who have ratified it, and the deposit of all instruments of ratification which may be effected subsequently.

DONE at Rome this 4th day of November 1950 in English and French, both texts being equally authentic, in a single copy which shall remain deposited in the archives of the Council of Europe. The Secretary-General shall transmit certified copies to each of the signatories.

Bibliography

SELECTED BIBLIOGRAPHY

Academy of Sciences of the U.S.S.R., Institute of Law. *International Law.*

American Law Institute. *Model Penal Code.*

Aristotle. *Politics and Poetics.*

Bentham, Jeremy. *Principles of Legislation.*

Brierly, J. L. *The Law of Nations.*

Caussade, J. P. de. *Self-Abandonment to Divine Providence.*

Calhoun, John C. *A Disquisition on Government.*

Chambers, William N. and Salisbury, Robert H. *Democracy in the Mid-Twentieth Century.*

Commager, Henry S. *Majority Rule and Minority Rights.*

Djilas, Milovan. *Die Neue Klasse.*

Engels, Friedrich. *Socialism, Utopian and Scientific.*

Feuerbach, Ludwig. *The Essence of Christianity.*

Fichte, Johann G. *Addresses to the German Nation.*

Franck, Thomas. *Race and Nationalism.*

Hayek, Friedrich. *The Road to Serfdom.*

Hegel, Georg W. F. *Lectures on the Philosophy of History. The Philosophy of Law.*

Hitler, Adolf. *Mein Kampf.*

Hobbes, Thomas. *Leviathan.*

Hook, Sidney. *Toward the Understanding of Karl Marx.*

Jefferson, Thomas. *Selected Letters.*

Khrushchev, Nikita S. *Crimes of the Stalin Era.*

Laski, Harold J. *State in Theory and Practice.*

Lauterpacht, H. *The Function of Law in the International Community.*

Lenin, Vladimir I. *Imperialism; the Highest Stage of Capitalism. State and Revolution. The Teachings of Karl Marx.*

Leonhard, Wolfgang. *Die Revolution entlaesst ihre Kinder.*

Locke, John. *The Second Treatise of Government.*

Machiavelli, Niccolo. *The Prince.*

Mao Tse-tung. *On People's Democratic Dictatorship.*

Marx, Karl. *Das Kapital.*

Marx, Karl and Engels, Friedrich. *Deutsche Ideologie. Manifest der Kommunistischen Partei. der Kommunistischen Partei.*

McKitterick, T.E.M. and Younger, Kenneth. *Fabian International Essays.*

Mehnert, Klaus. *Der Sowjetmensch.*

Mill, John Stuart. *On Liberty.*

Palmieri, Mario. *The Philosophy of Fascism.*

Plato. *The Republic.*

   The Laws.

Pipes, Richard. *The Russian Intelligentsia.*

Remec, Peter P. *The Position of the Individual in International Law according to Grotius and Vattel.*

Rosenberg, Alfred. *The Myth of the Twentieth Century.*

Rousseau, Jean Jacques. *The Social Contract.*

Stalin, J. W. *The Foundations of Leninism.*

Schumpeter, Joseph A. *Imperialism and Social Classes.*

Stevenson, Adlai E. *Speeches.*

Teilhard de Chardin, Pierre. *The Phenomenon of Man.*

Tocqueville, Alexis de. *Democracy in America.*

Treitschke, Heinrich von. *Politics.*

Vetter, Gustav. *Dialectical Materialism.*

Wallace, Henry A. *Toward World Peace.*

Index